What Your Colleagues Are Saying . . .

"Nancy Frey, Douglas Fisher, and John Almarode have expertly created an insightful, timely, practical playbook for teachers and school leaders who want to learn more ways to ensure that all students gain skills using supportive structures called scaffolds. Most of all, educators will enjoy the techniques for using ongoing formative assessment and spiraling curriculum."

—**Virginia Kelsen,** Lead Human Resources Administrator,
El Rancho Unified School District

"At a time when every educator and transformational leader is strategizing on how to eliminate inequities and achievement gaps among their scholars, this book is a valuable, timely resource. The authors have masterfully defined the characteristics of effective scaffolding to make instruction and learning both accessible and relevant for all learners, regardless of the level they begin. I view this playbook as an absolute necessity—for its clarity and focus on the steps educators can take to help all scholars reach their highest academic potential."

—**Dana Trevethan,** Superintendent,
Turlock Unified School District

"How Scaffolding Works is a highly engaging and thought-provoking resource for school administrators, instructional coaches, and teachers to collaboratively learn about scaffolding. Each module includes real-life examples, opportunities for peer discussion, and an easy-to-use framework for deliberately planning scaffolds for *all* learners throughout the learning process. This playbook is a must-read for anyone wanting to learn how to use high effect-size strategies to scaffold learning."

—**Alisa Barret,** Director of Instruction,
Greenfield Exempted Village Schools

"This text provides a fresh lens through which to view the practice of scaffolding, applicable to all grade bands and subject areas!"

—**Tiffany Coleman,** Former Chair of Literacy Instruction,
Georgia Gwinnett College

"This playbook is a perfect next step after reading *The Teacher Clarity Playbook* and *The Success Criteria Playbook*. Nancy Frey, Douglas Fisher, and John Almarode continue to build on the importance of clear learning targets and success criteria because knowing what success will look or sound like helps teachers navigate handling the tricky parts as a student learns. When you know where a student is and where they need to go, you can easily make decisions about scaffolding."

—**Melanie Kosko,** K–8 Literacy Coordinator, Oak Ridge Schools

HOW
SCAFFOLDING WORKS

Nancy Frey | Douglas Fisher | John Almarode

HOW
SCAFFOLDING WORKS
a playbook
for Supporting and Releasing Responsibility to Students

CORWIN
Fisher & Frey

FOR INFORMATION:

Corwin
A SAGE Company
2455 Teller Road
Thousand Oaks, California 91320
(800) 233-9936
www.corwin.com

SAGE Publications Ltd.
1 Oliver's Yard
55 City Road
London EC1Y 1SP
United Kingdom

SAGE Publications India Pvt. Ltd.
B 1/I 1 Mohan Cooperative Industrial Area
Mathura Road, New Delhi 110 044
India

SAGE Publications Asia-Pacific Pte. Ltd.
18 Cross Street #10-10/11/12
China Square Central
Singapore 048423

Printed in the United States of America

ISBN 978-1-0719-0415-2

President: Mike Soules
Vice President and Editorial
   Director: Monica Eckman
Director and Publisher, Corwin
   Classroom: Lisa Luedeke
Associate Content Development
   Editor: Sarah Ross
Production Editor: Melanie Birdsall
Typesetter: C&M Digitals (P) Ltd.
Proofreader: Scott Oney
Cover Designer: Rose Storey
Marketing Manager: Megan Naidl

This book is printed on acid-free paper.

23 24 25 26 27 10 9 8 7 6 5 4 3 2 1

Contents

Visit the companion website at
resources.corwin.com/howscaffoldingworks
for downloadable resources.

Acknowledgments

Corwin gratefully acknowledges the contributions of the following reviewers:

Lydia Bagley
Instructional Support Specialist
Cobb County School District
Marietta, GA

Tiffany Coleman
Former Chair of Literacy Instruction
Georgia Gwinnett College
Loganville, GA

Introduction

In September 1932, at the height of the Great Depression, a photographer snapped a photograph of 11 ironworkers sharing and enjoying their lunches and cigarettes.

This picture has found its place as one of the most iconic and recognizable photographs in the United States (e.g., *100 Photographs: The Most Influential Images of All Time;* Time, 2016). You likely have seen this photograph and, regardless of the number of times you view this picture, have a reaction to the idea that these men are suspended 70 floors above Manhattan without any support or safety equipment. These men worked daily to build a 587-foot-tall (179 meters) skyscraper, but only with the help of a scaffolding system. Like all scaffoldings, there are three main components: standards, ledgers, and transoms.

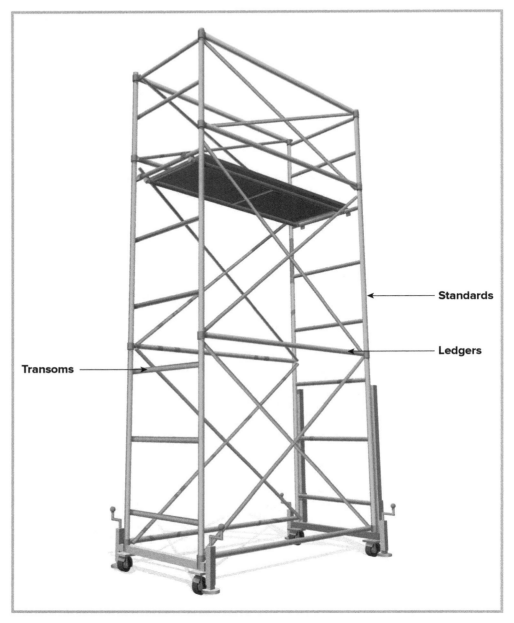

Source: Graphic courtesy of iStock.com/Sussenn

What does this have to do with this playbook, a playbook on scaffolding? To answer this question, let's turn our attention to the definition of scaffolding. What exactly is meant by *scaffolding*?

Scaffolding is a support system or structure. This supporting framework is temporary and movable, allowing individuals to move forward in whatever task is at hand. What is important to note here is that there is an essential relationship between the scaffolding and the specific task at hand:

1. Scaffolding is only used when the task at hand is not possible to complete without that support system or structure.

2. Scaffolding is customized (i.e., movable) based on the specific needs of the individuals engaged in the task; there is no one-size-fits-all scaffolding.

3. Scaffolding is used until the support system or structure is no longer needed; scaffolds are temporary and not permanent.

> Take a moment and circle, underline, or highlight the term *temporary* in the third statement. You will need this term again very soon.

This is a playbook about the scaffolding of learning in our schools and classrooms. Instead of building skyscrapers, we are building self-regulated learners who take ownership of their learning. Instead of standards, ledgers, and transoms, we offer strategies, interventions, and different approaches. As we begin to uncover how scaffolding works, take a moment and reflect on the three relationships between scaffolding and tasks.

Relationship Between Scaffolding and Tasks	What does this make me think of in my own school or classroom?
Scaffolding is only used when the task at hand is not possible to complete without that support system or structure.	
Scaffolding is customized (i.e., movable) based on the specific needs of the individuals engaged in the task; there is no one-size-fits-all scaffolding.	
Scaffolding is used until the support system or structure is no longer needed; scaffolds are temporary and not permanent.	

Scaffolding tasks, whether those tasks are the construction of a skyscraper or tasks in our schools and classrooms, are absolutely essential in the successful completion of the tasks. However, scaffolding is not as easy as connecting standards, ledgers, and transoms. Consider the following questions that must be considered when putting up, moving, and taking down. In the extra space provided, add your own questions about scaffolding. What questions do you have for your own teaching and learning?

- When do I set up the scaffolding?

- How much scaffolding is needed?

- How do I know when and where to move the scaffolding?

- When do I remove the scaffolding?

-

-

-

-

-

The questions we provided, along with those questions you added to the list, will serve as our learning goals in this playbook. From time to time, you will be prompted to return to this list and check in with your progress in answering these questions.

Throughout the pages of this playbook, we will look at different examples from primary, elementary, middle school, and high school content, skills, practices, dispositions, and understandings. Scaffolding can and should be a part of teaching and learning in every school and classroom. This requires that we collaborate with our colleagues to generate, gather, and make sense of the evidence about our students' learning. This evidence is what helps us answer the above questions.

COLLABORATE TO SCAFFOLD

Each module offers you an opportunity for learning how scaffolding works, practicing the "putting up, moving, and taking down" of scaffolds with different grade-level and content areas, and, finally, applying the learning to your own school and classroom. We encourage you to engage in this playbook by circling, highlighting, underlining, writing in your own notes and responses, and using sticky notes to mark pages. Most importantly, though, we encourage you to collaborate with your colleagues. Although using this playbook as part of your personal learning is fine, the opportunity to dialogue about scaffolding and collaborate on how to use scaffolding to accelerate learning is best done collectively with colleagues. We offer three suggestions for collaborating with colleagues:

➤ Work with an accountability partner

➤ Work with an instructional coach

➤ Work with a group of others during your common planning or PLC+ meeting (see Fisher et al., 2020)

Let's start with **accountability partners**. The use of this playbook during common planning or your PLC+ meeting may not be feasible. You may be more comfortable partnering with a colleague across the hall, in another part of the building, or in another school. You and this colleague can move through the modules, engage in the tasks, implement ideas in your own classrooms, and debrief the impact this had on advancing student learning. You and this colleague will serve as accountability partners in increasing your effectiveness at scaffolding learning for your students.

A second way to work collaboratively through this playbook is to work alongside an **instructional coach**. Instructional coaches provide all of us with an outside perspective on the teaching and learning in our classrooms. They can provide us with the right feedback at the right time. In fact, working with an instructional coach may offer the opportunity for the instructional coach to build their capacity by scaffolding to the instructional coaching cycle. After all, we have all needed our own professional learning scaffolded at some point in our careers. Either way, sitting down with an instructional coach, engaging in critical dialogue about supporting learners, developing specific scaffolds for your students, and then working together to evaluate the impact on student learning is an invaluable asset to professional growth.

Finally, this playbook can support your **work with a group of others** in collaborative conversations during your PLC+ meeting (Fisher et al., 2020). The work of this playbook is another tool for the work you do in your PLC+. The use of these five guiding questions of PLC+ will keep the focus relentlessly on the learning of our students:

➤ Where are we going?

➤ Where are we now?

➤ How do we move learning forward?

➤ What did we learn today?

➤ Who benefited and who did not benefit? (Fisher et al., 2020, p. 8)

In PLC+, teachers identify learning intentions and discuss ideas for instruction. They meet to review student work and figure out if their efforts have been fruitful. They also talk about students who need additional instruction or support for success. This is best done together, during our work as a community of learners.

I.1 HOW THIS PLAYBOOK SUPPORTS THE WORK OF PLC+

PLC Question	Module
Where are we going?	Module 5 focuses on goal setting and notes the value of knowing where we are going. In addition, Module 4 explores mental models of expertise, which are even bigger than the lesson goals we have for students.
Where are we now?	Module 7 focuses on front-end scaffolds and the ways in which we plan based on what students already know. In addition, Module 3 offers a model of scaffolding based on what we know about students and their current levels of understanding.
How do we move learning forward?	There are several modules that focus on moving learning forward, including Module 6 on deliberate practice to the four modules on scaffolding learning (Modules 7, 8, 9, and 10).
What did we learn today?	Having a clear understanding of what we learned today (both us and our learners) requires noticing what learners are saying and doing and communicating with them around their learning. Again Modules 7, 8, 9, and 10 provide evidence of students learning, and Module 11 focuses on fading scaffolds based on what students have learned.
Who benefited and who did not benefit?	While every module of this playbook applies to this particular question, the primary issue is around noticing which learners are giving, receiving, and integrating feedback. This is especially important in peer scaffolding, Module 10. If we do not take notice of how learners are engaging with the scaffolds provided, we may not know who benefited and who did not until it is too late.

Whether you have an accountability partner, access to an instructional coach, or a high-functioning, high-impact PLC+, the benefit of a collaborative approach is the opportunity to engage in critical dialogue around what scaffolding looks like for you and your learners. In fact, the need for a collaborative approach is highlighted by the very picture that started this conversation. There is more to the story in the photograph of the 11 ironworkers.

This photograph was staged. That's right, staged. The photographer did not naturally capture these 11 ironworkers dangling from the sixty-ninth story of the building swapping lunches and cigarettes. Instead, they were staged in a variety of poses to generate a photograph for advertising the building. Furthermore, the sturdy and reliable RCA building was right below them, outside of the view of the camera (Contrera, 2019). Again, staged. One of the challenges we must look out for during our work in this playbook is over-scaffolding. Unlike the photographer of this picture, we want to ensure that our scaffolds do not remove the productive struggle, lack the customization to meet the needs of our learners, or become a permanent fixture. If that happens, even if outside the field of vision of us as a teacher, we can create a complacency and slow down the progress of the learning. Instead, our singular focus must be to keep everything within our field of vision so that we can accelerate student learning.

Let's unpack *how scaffolding works*.

1

THE FOUNDATIONS OF SCAFFOLDING

LEARNING INTENTION

We are learning about the foundations of scaffolding so that we can better understand how scaffolding accelerates learning.

SUCCESS CRITERIA

We will know we are successful when

- We can define what is meant by scaffolding.
- We can identify the foundations of scaffolding.
- We can apply scaffolding to a common task in our lives.
- We can describe the reciprocal relationship involved in scaffolding.

In your own words, describe what is meant by scaffolding in your school or classroom. To support your thinking, use the following question stems to get you started.

- What is scaffolding in our schools and classrooms?

- Why would we want or need to scaffold?

- When do you think scaffolding is appropriate? When is it not appropriate?

(Continued)

(Continued)

- Who gets the scaffolds?

- How do you scaffold learning?

Hold on to your answers to these questions. They will help us later in this and upcoming modules.

Instructional scaffolding has been a part of teaching practices since at least 1976 when Wood, Bruner, and Ross coined the phrase. However, the idea of scaffolding is much, much older. We have been "scaffolding" learning experiences for students since there have been apprenticeship models of learning.

The apprenticeship model is used by teachers to support learners in a specific task. Learners work alongside teachers to develop proficiency in a specific skill that begins with the teacher *modeling* the skill. Through low-stakes tasks, the learner mimics the actions of the teacher and reflects on their own experience. This is called *approximating*. Over time, the learner begins to engage in higher-stakes tasks with the role of the teacher *fading* away. Finally, the learner performs the actual task independently, seeking assistance from the teacher when needed. This leads to *self-directed learning* and the student *applying* the learning to other situations.

Take a moment and identify specific ways you have used the apprenticeship model in your own classroom:

Modeling:

_____

_____

_____

Approximating:

_____

_____

Fading:

_____

_____

_____

Self-directed learning:

_____

_____

_____

Generalizing/applying:

_____

_____

_____

_____

Educators have always done more than simply relied on telling information to students. In other words, we scaffolded learning before the term *scaffolding* was ever used. Of course, we have learned a great deal in the years since the term *scaffolding* was first introduced.

The term *scaffolding* resonates with us because of the diversity we observe in our learners each and every day. From fractions to figurative language, physical geography to photosynthesis, or Renaissance Art to refinement cues, each of our students is at different points in their learning progression. Thus, supporting them in a way that offers them the opportunity to succeed is something we value and strive for in our classrooms. Yet, our most common experience with the term *scaffolding* is associated with construction sites or buildings.

Take a moment and flip back to the Introduction, page 3. There was a term you were asked to circle, underline, or highlight. That term is what fills in the next sentence in this playbook. Write that term in the spaces.

> A construction scaffold is a _____ structure for holding workers and materials during the erection, repair, or decoration of a building. Essentially, scaffolds extend the reach of the worker and provide access to places that would have been inaccessible without the _____ structures.

The term you just added to the previous sentences is very important to our work in this playbook: *temporary*. The point of any scaffold is to provide a temporary structure that is subsequently removed. Interestingly, contractors do not. It's also worth noting that we don't spend a lot of money on scaffolding to make them look pretty. The standards, ledgers, and transoms are not dressed up or painted. They are, however, closely monitored to ensure the safety and security of the workers.

The point of any scaffold is to provide a temporary structure that is subsequently removed.

Are you starting to see the direction we are headed in this playbook? Let's start jotting down our thinking up to this point. Using the Venn diagram below, compare and contrast construction scaffolding with instructional scaffolding. This is just the start of our thinking, and we can add to the Venn diagram later.

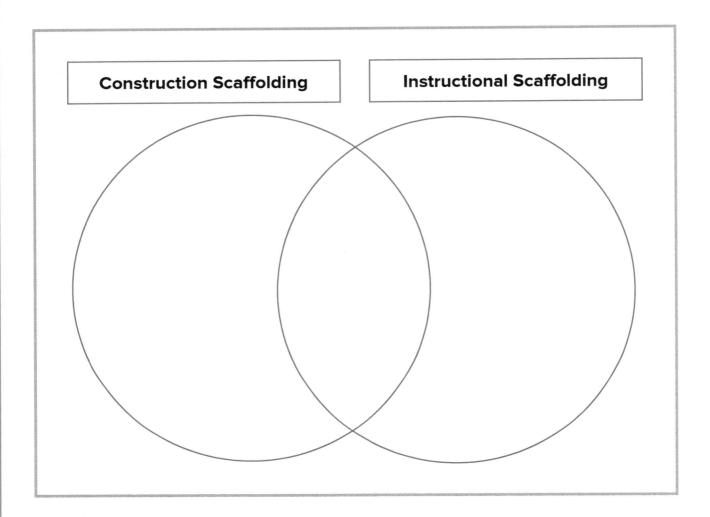

Let's consider a familiar example: teaching someone to ride a bicycle. Think about a time when you taught a child to ride a bike or when you observed another person teach a child to ride a bike. Make a list of the actions involved in this process in the following space.

Actions Taken to Teach Bike Riding

1.

2.

3.

4.

5.

6.

7.

We asked colleagues and friends to consider the same process and gathered their responses.

1. Used a smaller bike

2. Added training wheels

3. Added safety equipment (e.g., helmets, pads)

4. Held the back of the bike and ran behind

5. Encouraged the child

You may have had other items on your list, but let's analyze the lists a bit. Note that there are actions that "right-size" the experience. The bike was smaller to fit the child. Did you have items on your list that "right-sized" the experience? If so, mark those with an "R." There were temporary supports included on our list, such as training wheels or no pedals so that the child could touch the ground. Mark the temporary supports on your list with a "T." We also had items on our list that made sure that the child felt (and was) safe. For example, the adult handled the tricky parts as the child acquired other foundational skills. Mark the safety supports on your list with an "S." Finally, we encouraged and praised the progressive learning and performance. Mark those items associated with feedback on your list with an "F." You probably also remember the first time that you let go. The child turned their head to see you, moved the handlebars to the right or left, and promptly fell over. And what did you do after you checked to make sure that there were no injuries? You encouraged the child to get back on the bike and try again.

The items on our list and your list are part of a reciprocal relationship involved in teaching someone to ride a bike. This reciprocal relationship was illustrated by Malik (2017) (see Figure 1.1).

1.1 RECIPROCAL RELATIONSHIP IN SCAFFOLDING

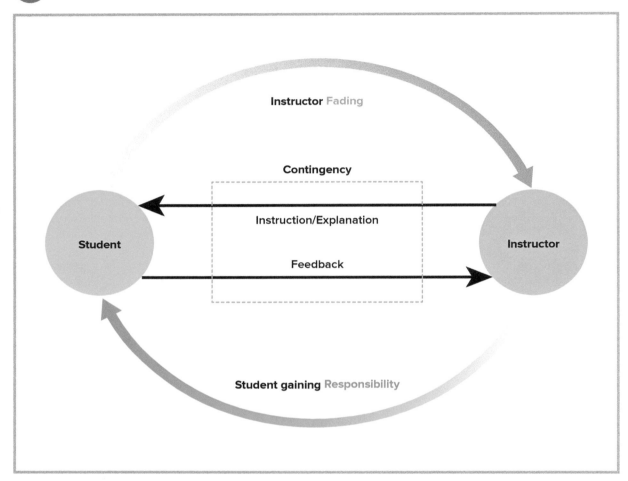

Source: Malik (2017).

Take a close look at the image of the two-gradient model developed by Shoaib Malik. Use the space below to summarize what you see in the model and what you believe the model communicates about instructional scaffolding. You may even want to add additional questions to the list on page 4 in the Introduction.

Now, let's start to tie all of this together. This reciprocal relationship forms the foundation for instructional scaffolding.

SCAFFOLDING FOUNDATIONS

There are some key takeaways from the example of teaching someone to ride a bike that apply to any situation where scaffolds are provided, including

 Right-sizing the task

 Making sure learning is a safe experience

 Handling the tricky parts as the student learns

 Providing encouragement, even when there are temporary failures

The success of scaffolding depends on the intensity, frequency, and duration of the scaffolds.

If you were lucky enough to teach a child to ride a bike, hopefully you are no longer running along behind them, holding the seat, and offering encouragement. Eventually, you faded your support as skills developed.

COACH A PEER

Talk with a peer about a task that was challenging for a learner or learners. Write that task at the top of the chart below and then discuss the questions below to learn more about how we try to scaffold learning.

DESCRIBE THE TASK	
How did you make sure learning was a safe experience?	
How did you handle the tricky parts as the student learns?	
How did you provide encouragement, even when there were temporary failures?	
How did you fade the supports?	

The evidence on instructional scaffolding is strong. There have been four meta-analyses on scaffolding, with an overall effect size of 0.58, which is an above-average influence and one that should accelerate learning (www.visiblelearningmetax.com). Of course, like many other influences, the success of scaffolding depends on the intensity, frequency, and duration of the scaffolds. In the hands of an expert educator, scaffolding is a powerful way to deepen learning.

CONCLUSION

Instructional scaffolds are an important strategy to ensure students' learning. There are several foundational aspects of scaffolding, including the idea that the scaffolds are temporary and should be faded.

Before moving on to the next module, we have provided a list of concepts explored thus far in the playbook.

➡ Instructional scaffolding

➡ Temporary

➡ Fading

➡ Right-sizing

Flip back through Module 1 and the Introduction and add additional concepts to the list.

➡

➡

➡

➡

➡

Using the terms listed on the previous page, summarize your learning using ***all*** of the terms. Make sure your summary highlights the relationships between these terms and does not simply repeat their definitions (e.g., purposeful practice, *not* naive practice).

Scaffolding requires learners to engage in deliberate practice.

However, there is one part of scaffolding that we are missing. Scaffolding requires learners to engage in deliberate practice. We will turn our attention to the importance and role of practicing very soon. Before we do that, let's look at the history of scaffolding. Knowing the origin of scaffolding and the research behind this important aspect of teaching and learning provides the foundation for *how scaffolding works* in our schools and classrooms.

SELF-ASSESSMENT

Before moving forward, consider the success criteria for this module. You will notice these statements have been revised from "We can" statements to "Can I?" questions. Using the traffic light scale, with red being not confident, yellow being somewhat confident, and green indicating very confident, how confident are you in your understanding of the foundations of scaffolding? You'll also want to take note of evidence you have for your self-assessment.

SUCCESS CRITERIA	SELF-ASSESSMENT	EVIDENCE
Can I define what is meant by scaffolding?		
Can I identify the foundations of scaffolding?		
Can I apply scaffolding to a common task in our lives?		
Can I describe the reciprocal relationship involved in scaffolding?		

Access resources, tools, and guides
for this module at the companion website:
resources.corwin.com/howscaffoldingworks

2

THE ORIGINS OF SCAFFOLDING

LEARNING INTENTION

We are learning about the research behind scaffolding so that we can better address our concerns about the use of scaffolding in our classrooms.

SUCCESS CRITERIA

We will know we are successful when

- We can describe how we know that scaffolding is beneficial to learning.
- We can explain the aspects of scaffolding discovered in the research.
- We can identify concerns, challenges, or barriers with scaffolding learning.
- We can discuss how scaffolding is related to engagement.

Where did the idea of scaffolding originate? What are the components of scaffolding that we should consider? Use the following question stems to jump-start your thinking.

- What is needed for scaffolding to work?

- How do we keep students engaged when learning? What role might scaffolding play?

Thus far, we have provided mostly non-academic examples to build our shared understanding of scaffolding. But our work involves academic content, including a wide range of skills, concepts, and understandings that students need to learn if they are to be successful in their future pursuits. Wood et al. (1976) define scaffolding as "a process that enables a child or novice to solve a task or achieve a goal that would be beyond his unassisted efforts" (p. 90). A current working definition of scaffolding in academics comes from the IRIS Center and reads:

> *Instructional scaffolding* is a process through which a teacher adds supports for students in order to enhance learning and aid in the mastery of tasks. The teacher does this by systematically building on students' experiences and knowledge as they are learning new skills. Just like [a scaffold], these supports are temporary and adjustable. As students master the assigned tasks, the supports are gradually removed. (Iris Center, n.d.)

> Take a moment and circle, underline, or highlight key words or phrases from this definition. Then, describe how this definition is similar and different from the earlier definition presented in the Introduction on page 2.

Instructional scaffolding sounds easy, right? Anyone who has ever tried to scaffold the learning of another knows that it is not and will not be easy. As Wood (1998) noted, "Monitoring children's activity, remembering what one has said or done to prompt that activity, and responding quickly to their efforts at an appropriate level is a demanding intellectual feat. Effective teaching is as difficult as the learning it seeks to promote" (p. 164). And that's why we have decided to tackle this subject. As we have noted, the term *scaffolding,* or *instructional scaffolding,* was coined by Wood et al. (1976). In the first part of this module, we'll review their ground-breaking study. Later in this module, we'll explore concerns about scaffolding and newer research on scaffolding.

However, we need to first return to our earlier work and review our previous responses.

> Take a moment and flip back to the beginning of Module 1, page 7. You were asked to describe what is meant by scaffolding in your school or classroom. Take some time to edit or revise your earlier responses in light of the definition provided by the IRIS Center. What additional information can you now add to your earlier response? Is there anything you need to change so that your earlier response is more precise, accurate, and robust?

THE PREREQUISITE CONDITION FOR SCAFFOLDING

In their study with young children, Wood, Bruner, and Ross noted that learners could not benefit from scaffolding unless "one paramount condition is fulfilled" (p. 90). That condition requires that students understand that there is a viable solution to the problem or situation they have encountered. That makes it sound like surface-level learning, but we must be careful. Yes, educators can scaffold students' acquisition of concepts and skills early in the learning process. But educators can also scaffold students' deep learning experiences. In the words of Wood et al., the learner "must be able to *recognize* a solution to a particular class of problems before he is himself able to produce the steps leading to it without assistance" (p. 90, emphasis in original). Note that they say a solution to a particular *class* of problems, rather than the solution to a specific problem. In other words, scaffolding is not limited to students figuring out the answer to a specific task, but rather learning how to think about a type of challenge that they have been given.

This is an important point as scaffolding cannot be reduced to pushing students to the right answers and avoiding incorrect ones. We have all learned from our incorrect responses, faulty thinking, and the errors we have made. Rather, scaffolding should develop students' thinking habits and result in transfer, or the application of knowledge and skills to unique situations.

Deliberate practice is based on a mental model of expertise. In other words, does the person engaged in the practice know what it will look like once mastered?

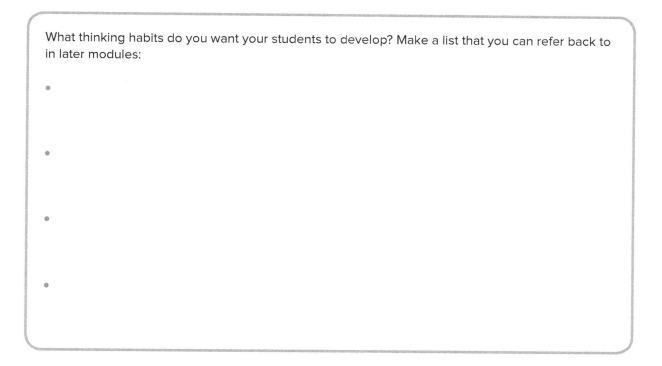

What thinking habits do you want your students to develop? Make a list that you can refer back to in later modules:

-
-
-
-

But it starts with students' ability to recognize that there is a solution to the cognitive challenge in front of them. That challenge may be decoding a word or writing an argument. It may involve simple arithmetic or inferential statistics. And it may involve addressing challenges for which there are no clear-cut "right" answers, such as creating art or giving a speech. Scaffolding can be used to support learner performance in any of these situations, provided that the learner knows that there is a solution, even if that means that there are multiple ways to demonstrate success.

As we will see in the next module, deliberate practice is based on a mental model of expertise. In other words, does the person engaged in the practice know what it will look like once mastered?

Your turn: Consider a learning task you have for your learners. This should be different from the learning task in Module 1. What would your students need to know to solve the problem? In other words, make a list of concepts, skills, and understandings that learners must know, understand, and be able to do to arrive at a solution.

This list will help us construct a mental model of expertise, just like Horacio. In our case, we have to ensure that we devote time and attention to unpacking the task, identifying the concepts, skills, and understandings, so that we can clearly provide a mental model for our learners. This ensures the prerequisite condition is present for scaffolding in our classroom.

In your own words, write the prerequisite condition that must be present for scaffolding to be successful in our classrooms.

Now let's look at the aspects of scaffolding.

SIX SCAFFOLDING FUNCTIONS

Based on their data, Wood et al. identified six scaffolding functions or aspects that they believed should be considered when supporting students to complete tasks. The first function likely occurs at the outset of the learning experience, but the others are more recursive in nature. We'll explore each of the six functions and analyze a classroom experience.

1. **Recruitment.** The first task in scaffolding is to solicit students' interest in the task. The teacher must ensure that students see *relevance* in the activity or assignment and *understand the requirements of the task*. It's hard to scaffold when students don't care about what they are expected to learn or if they have no idea what the task requires.

2. **Reduction in degrees of freedom.** This requires that teachers *simplify the task* by reducing the number of acts or steps to reach a solution. When teachers have engaged in task analysis, they understand the steps and process, which can then be used to reduce the options, thereby allowing a focus on the steps required to be successful.

3. **Direction maintenance.** Learning is often not a linear process, but much more like sailing in which you tack and jibe to get to the destination. Without guidance, students may head in a wrong direction, lose interest, or even give up. Thus, part of scaffolding is to "*keep them in pursuit of a particular objective*" (Wood et al., p. 98).

4. **Marking critical features.** As part of the support provided, those providing scaffolding *highlight some features of the task*. This includes *noting actions that had an impact* so that the learner is likely to try that again, as well as noting the discrepancy between what the learner did and what might be a more correct response.

5. **Frustration control.** As Wood et al. noted, "*Problem solving should be less dangerous or stressful with a tutor than without*" (p. 98). As such, the person providing the scaffolding can provide some "face-saving" comments for the student who is struggling or offer additional prompts and cues that support success. However, the risk here is creating too much dependency on the person offering scaffolds.

6. **Demonstration.** Modeling, thinking aloud, and providing other types of input *allow the student an opportunity to imitate the actions of another*, which may resolve the temporary block in the successful completion of the task.

Pause for a moment and review the six aspects of scaffolding.

Could you explain these to a colleague?

Could you provide examples to clarify the meaning of each aspect?

Find a colleague and find out. Get feedback from them and fine-tune your explanations and examples. Yes, this is deliberate practice.

Now let's look at an example in the context of a classroom. However, we are going to ask you to actively read this example. Circle, underline, or highlight information or details you think are most important from this example.

At the start of the class, Kim Chan-Patino asks students to complete a few problems that provide information about what students need to learn next. As students enter, Ms. Chan-Patino says, "Today, we will apply what we learned about the distributive property to *both* sides of the equation. It's not about speed, remember, but we are learning to think about these problems and what they really mean. Learning to solve these equations allows us to eventually make predictions and then we can use those predictions to make decisions."

Before inviting students to solve problems on their own, Ms. Chan-Patino walked to a dry-erase board with a problem written on it—$14(x + 1) = 14x$—saying, "This one only requires that I use the distributed property on one side. And I must remember to *distribute* the 14 to both the x and the 1 (drawing arrows from the 14 to the x and to the 1). Once I have distributed, I know how to solve for x. Here's a problem for you: $2(x + 12) = 4(x + 4)$."

Ms. Chan-Patino visited Sofia first, asking, "How will you start?" Sofia responded that she needed to distribute the 2 first and got started.

Ms. Chan-Patino then visited Carlos, who was staring at the problem, and said, "Maybe you should start by drawing the line down the center at the equal sign. That's what we did last week, remember?" Carlos gets started.

Ms. Chan-Patino notices that Felix has completed the left side but did not fully distribute the 4 on the right side. In response, she says, "Let's check again. Did you use the arrow method we talked about?"

Ms. Chan-Patino continues to walk around the room, providing support so that students continue to persevere in problem solving. She makes several comments aloud, such as "I'm seeing people add or subtract the same thing from both sides." She also says, "This is the first time we've had a problem that required us to distribute on both sides of the equation." A few minutes later, she says, "Let's pause there. I'd like to do one more as an example and we'll identify key steps. Then you can use those steps to check your own work."

Ms. Chan-Patino explains how she solves a new problem, identifying the process at each step. She then asks students to use the steps to review their work. Ms. Chan-Patino ends the lesson by asking students to think about this:

> I have 5 friends and we're going to the movies. I need to know how much it will cost for all of us to go. The admission price is $12.00, and we want popcorn which is $5.00. How will you set up the equation?

Your circling, underlining, or highlighting was purposeful. Let's put your active reading to work. What did you see?

Did you see any of the functions that Wood et al. (1976) identified?

Use the chart to extract evidence of each aspect of scaffolding from Ms. Chan-Patino's classroom.

Factor	Evidence From Ms. Chan-Patino
Recruitment	
Reduction in degrees of freedom	
Direction maintenance	
Marking critical features	
Frustration control	
Demonstration	

COACH A PEER

This feature is an opportunity for you to try out new learning. We'll give you a short scenario about a teacher whose instruction might benefit from scaffolding:

The students in Marco Rincon's class will use graphic organizers to prepare for an upcoming project. The students have learned a lot but need to organize their bits of information so that they can use it later. Mr. Rincon starts by saying, "We have the next 15 minutes to get ourselves organized. I'd like you to take your notes and get them synthesized down to a page so that you see the connections between all of the different ideas. You can use any of the graphic organizers that we have studied to help you. Then we will do our escape room puzzle, and remember the rules—you can only use your one-pager."

Mr. Rincon creates escape room-like puzzles for students to solve using the content of the class. He continues, "Our next puzzle has never been solved at this school. We can do it, right? [Yes!] But we need to have our information organized so that we can easily find it."

How might Mr. Rincon use the scaffolding functions to support students?

FACTOR	RECOMMENDATION FOR MR. RINCON
Recruitment	
Reduction in degrees of freedom	
Direction maintenance	
Marking critical features	
Frustration control	
Demonstration	

You might have noticed that Ms. Chan-Patino and Mr. Rincon's students were engaged in their learning. One of the benefits of instructional scaffolding is authentic engagement, engagement across multiple dimensions of learning.

INSTRUCTIONAL SCAFFOLDING AS ENGAGEMENT

Educational psychologists often describe engagement in three dimensions: *metacognitive, cognitive*, and *affective*. These form the heart of motivation for learning. But they also provide a lens for understanding the further development of instructional scaffolding as a field.

> What do you think of when you hear metacognitive engagement, cognitive engagement, and affective engagement? Use the space below to summarize what you believe is meant by these terms.

Metacognition in scaffolding. Metacognitive scaffolds are intended to build students' ability to think about their thinking, which is a key skill for self-regulation and the future ability to apply the skills being taught. For example, there are times when students need *direction maintenance* because they have moved into a less productive route. Direction maintenance is more than redirection. Redirection is pointing students to a different path but without the reasoning that goes with it, for instance, when a teacher says, "You said that you wanted to use a startling statistic but I think you've asked a question of your reader instead." Direction maintenance that asks students to think metacognitively looks more like this: "I'd like for you to read aloud what you just wrote. Is it accomplishing what you intended? In other words, are you meeting the goal that you set for yourself to startle the reader?"

Cognition in scaffolding. Cognitive structuring and *reduction of degrees of freedom* form the heart of instructional scaffolding. This entails the give-and-take of learning as students and the teacher respond to one another. To do so most effectively requires *dynamic assessment*, which is to say that there is an iterative loop of test-teach-retest.

For example, a teacher working with a student on reading multisyllabic words asks a child to identify the vowels in a multisyllabic word to see if the child can locate the syllables (test). The teacher then reminds the student that all syllables contain a vowel (teach), then asks the student to segment the word (retest). The teacher then points out that the syllables can be read like small words (teach) and then has the student read each syllable in succession (retest). When the child does so successfully, they are then prompted by the teacher to read the syllables more rapidly to pronounce them as an entire word (teach). They work through each multisyllabic word on the list.

When the student has difficulty, the teacher moves into reducing the degrees of freedom. When the child stumbles on *transportation* due to an incorrect method for identifying the syllables, she covers the letters at the beginning and end of the longer word with blank cards and asks if there is a smaller word in there that could stand alone. With the reduced view, the student could see the word "port."

"Can that be a single syllable?" the teacher asks.

"Yes, because a syllable has a vowel," says the child, now rewriting the four syllables in the longer word. By covering the rest of the word, the teacher was able to temporarily isolate a specific skill in order to rebuild student knowledge.

Affect in scaffolding. The feelings and emotions of the student are crucial in whether they will learn or not. It comes as no surprise that students who are uninterested, overwhelmed, or frustrated are going to shut down. Recruitment and frustration control are critical for preventing or restoring learning during scaffolding. Affective scaffolding has received increased attention in this decade, especially in the instruction of multilingual learners. Affective scaffolds are used with intention to foster the emotional safety needed to learn. These can include (Tajeddin & Kamali, 2020):

➡ *Encouraging*: Providing acknowledgments like "aha," "okay," and "good" to spur the learner to continue.

➡ *Emotional scaffolding*: Providing feedback on the content of the learner's talk to put them in a relaxed condition or using analogies, metaphors, and stories to influence students' emotional response to the content. For example, the teacher might offer support by saying, "We can do hard things; we've done it before." Or the teacher may use a story, such as "I remember a time a few weeks ago when you got frustrated and you had some ways to work through that, right?"

➡ *Shy tracking*: Inviting a student who has a low willingness to communicate to contribute as might be the case when a teacher says privately to a student, "This is a really good idea. Would you mind sharing with the class?"

These affective scaffolds don't have a direct causal link to academic learning, but rather are interspersed as invitations and encouragements. These are critical because effective instructional scaffolding is relational and bidirectional, and not a matter of demanding student performance of an academic skill or concept.

In 2010, van de Pol and colleagues engaged in a review of the previous decade's research on the subject, 66 studies in total. They investigated how instructional scaffolding was described, utilized, and analyzed. They developed a model of understanding how instructional scaffolding moves, or decisions by the teacher, might be analyzed, according to their intention (see Figure 2.1). *Intention* describes whether the scaffolding is meant to support metacognitive, cognitive, or affective engagement. In doing so, they built on the work of Wood et al. (1976) and others. Importantly, van de Pol and his colleagues wove the language of engagement into scaffolding.

The feelings and emotions of the student are crucial in whether they will learn or not.

2.1   A FRAMEWORK FOR ANALYSIS OF SCAFFOLDING STRATEGIES

	Scaffolding Intentions				
	Support of students' metacognitive activities	Support of students' cognitive activities		Support of student affect	
	A. Direction maintenance	B. Cognitive structuring	C. Reduction of degrees of freedom	D. Recruitment	E. Contingency management/ frustration control
Means 1. Feeding back 2. Hints 3. Instructing 4. Explaining 5. Modeling 6. Questioning					

Source: van de Pol et al. (2010, p. 278).

CONCERNS ABOUT SCAFFOLDING

Over the years since Wood et al. published their account of scaffolding, concerns have arisen about their model. We will discuss five of those concerns here:

1. **Limited ages are represented in their study.** First, it should be noted that they studied three-, four-, and five-year-olds building block pyramids. Interestingly, they noted significant differences in the ways in which scaffolding worked across these three years of life with reductions in the ratio between showing and telling with higher levels of showing for younger students. They also noted increased success with scaffolds as students get older. Thus, a valid question concerns the implications and application for older students in academic learning. Since 1976, there have been hundreds of studies of scaffolding and it seems safe to say that the general model applies to many, or even most, types of learning.

2. **The structure of the lessons.** The study that produced the evidence used to argue for scaffolding was based on individual interactions between an adult and a child. There were no other students waiting for something to happen and the adult did not have to manage groups of students at the same time.

This remains a challenge as many examples of scaffolding focus on individual students receiving support from a teacher. There are also examples of small-group scaffolded instruction, but it is rare to see whole-class examples. This makes sense given that the scaffolds needed by one student may not be necessary for another. More recent work on scaffolding includes front-end scaffolds that the teacher designs for the entire class in advance of the lesson. These will be discussed in Module 7.

3. **The learning they studied had only one right answer** (Wood et al.). There was only one way to build the pyramid that would work. In much of school-based learning, there are many right answers or many ways to get to the answer. This requires a sophisticated type of scaffolding and the use of heuristics, or a general cognitive framework that we rely on to reach a solution. Consider how you find a parking place. Do you want to park as close as possible to the place you are going? Are you looking for shade? Do you want to be away from other cars, if possible, to prevent your car from being scratched? Or do you take the first spot you see, congratulating yourself that you found one? There is no right way, but you likely have a heuristic for solving the parking spot problem. To ensure that students develop cognitive flexibility, creativity, and entrepreneurial spirit, teacher scaffolding needs to include heuristics, while recognizing the many right ways to do this.

4. **Is the teacher leading the student to a specific answer?** The role of the student has become important in the conversation about scaffolding. The concern is that the teacher is leading the student to a specific answer or kind of thinking. As Searle noted in "Scaffolding: Who's Building Whose Building?" (1984): "Schools . . . are rarely effective in allowing children either to initiate topics or to shape the experience for themselves. As a result, scaffolding can more often become the imposition of a structure on the student" (p. 481). Just eight years after the seminal piece on scaffolding was published, concerns about teachers using scaffolding to control students and their learning were raised. Others have raised concerns about the lack of a transactional relationship between teacher and students if instructional scaffolding is used too narrowly and excludes what the learners bring to the learning. Moll (1990) noted that learning is a "social system within which we hope children will learn, with the understanding that the social system is mutually and actively created by teachers and students" (p. 11). There is a danger that scaffolds can become reductionist and behavioristic and limit the child's role in co-constructing learning. In doing so, we thwart student ownership of learning and inhibit the transfer of learning. As we have noted elsewhere (e.g., Frey et al., 2018), students should be taught to take increased responsibility for their learning. At the same time, educators need to provide experiences that increase students' confidence and competence in the curriculum.

5. **A concern is that scaffolding has become excessive.** There is a concern that scaffolding has become excessive to the point that struggle has been removed from school. Students deserve an opportunity to grapple with ideas and information. They need to wallow a bit in the learning pit (Nottingham,

2017) and they need to experience productive success and failure (Kapur, 2016). We think you'll agree that much of the struggle has been removed from learning; that we pre-teach and frontload too much. While we reduce those forms of scaffolding, let's not forget that repeated failures without learning may result in a fixed mindset about certain topics and a future resistance to learning. It's more about supporting learners in the process of learning rather than removing the struggle.

 ## Use What You Know

Take a moment and review the five concerns around scaffolding. There is likely one of these concerns that reflects your own thoughts and feelings or the thoughts and feelings of your colleagues. Focus on that concern for now. Use the space below to draft a response to this concern that uses the features and characteristics of your context (e.g., your school, content area, grade level, or classroom). How would you respond to this concern?

CONCLUSION

Scaffolding was introduced several decades ago and has continued to be studied as an approach to supporting students' learning. The foundations of scaffolding, including the idea that students need to know that a solution is possible and what success looks like, still resonate today. That said, there are newer innovations in scaffolding that should be incorporated into the mix. In doing so, educators need to address the unintended consequences and challenges of scaffolding, including the risk of removing the struggle from learning. It's a balancing act: we must develop complex tasks and contingent plans to scaffold such that students struggle through the experience and learn along the way.

SELF-ASSESSMENT

Before moving forward, consider the success criteria for this module. You will notice these statements have been revised from "We can" statements to "Can I?" questions. Using the traffic light scale, with red being not confident, yellow being somewhat confident, and green indicating very confident, how confident are you in your new learning about the origins of scaffolding? You'll also want to take note of evidence you have for your self-assessment.

SUCCESS CRITERIA	SELF-ASSESSMENT	EVIDENCE
Can I describe how I know scaffolding is beneficial to learning?		
Can I explain the aspects of scaffolding discovered in the research?		
Can I identify concerns, challenges, or barriers with scaffolding learning?		
Can I discuss how scaffolding is related to engagement?		

Access resources, tools, and guides
for this module at the companion website:
resources.corwin.com/howscaffoldingworks

3

A MODEL FOR HOW SCAFFOLDING WORKS

We are learning about the contingencies necessary for making scaffolding work.

We will know we are successful when

- We can describe what is meant by contingencies in scaffolding.
- We can describe a model for implementing scaffolding in our schools and classrooms.
- We can support our scaffolding model with the research on instructional scaffolding.

We will share a framework or model for scaffolding in this module. What components are you already considering as you think about a model? Use the following question stems to jump-start your thinking.

- What role do goals play in scaffolding?

- What types of scaffolds can we use?

Over the past two modules, we have unpacked what is meant by scaffolding and why we need scaffolding, as well as explored the foundations, prerequisites, and concerns with scaffolding. Let's take a moment to review the big ideas and ensure we are comfortable with these foundational concepts and understandings. Yes, we are scaffolding our work in this module.

Take a moment and write down your initial responses to the following questions. After that, flip back to the Introduction and the first two modules to check your responses. Then, using a different type or color writing utensil, revise and edit your responses. We will revisit the edits and revisions very soon. For now, just make sure your original responses are discernable from your edits and revisions.

1. What is scaffolding or how would you define scaffolding?

2. Below, apply all **four** of the foundations of scaffolding to baking a cake.

Word Bank

Contingency

Explanation

Fading

Feedback

Instruction

Instructor

Responsibility

Student

3. Review the five concerns about scaffolding, relating them to the baking of a cake.

4. Finally, review the diagram on the next page and fill in the missing labels. We have provided an optional word bank in the margin. By the way, this is an example of a scaffold.

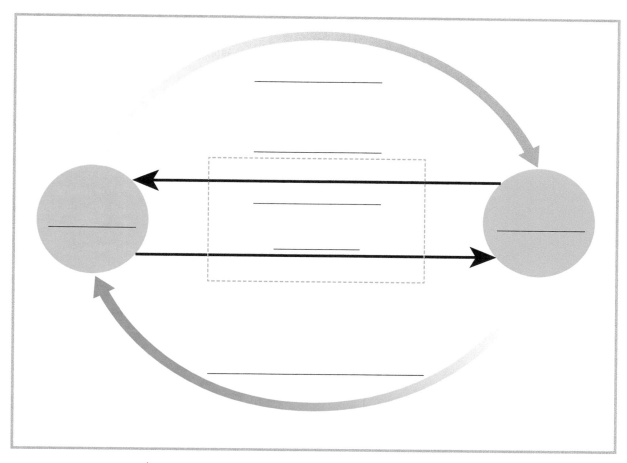

Source: Adapted from Malik (2017).

In this module, we want to pull out our magnifying glasses and take an up-close look at the contingency aspect of Malik's model. Contingency implies that "something" is possible but depends on other variables or circumstances. Take for example a contingency clause in a contract; *if this, then that*. This clause asserts that if certain conditions are met, then some specific outcome will happen. Flip back to page 12 in Module 1. Let's convert the four foundations of scaffolding into a contingency statement. If we do these four foundational things, then the probability of riding a bike goes up:

➡ Right-size the task

➡ Make sure learning is a safe experience

➡ Handle the tricky parts as the student learns

➡ Provide encouragement even when there are temporary failures

Yes, there is a lot going on in that quadrilateral marked contingency. What's inside that quadrilateral is *how scaffolding works* and the focus of this playbook.

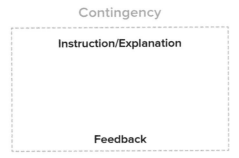

What are those instructional contingencies between the teacher and the learner? How do they result in teacher fading and increased learner responsibility? What is the role of feedback in scaffolding?

From our work in schools and classrooms, along with the body of research on scaffolding, we have developed a model for *how scaffolding works* (Figure 3.1).

 MODEL FOR HOW SCAFFOLDING WORKS

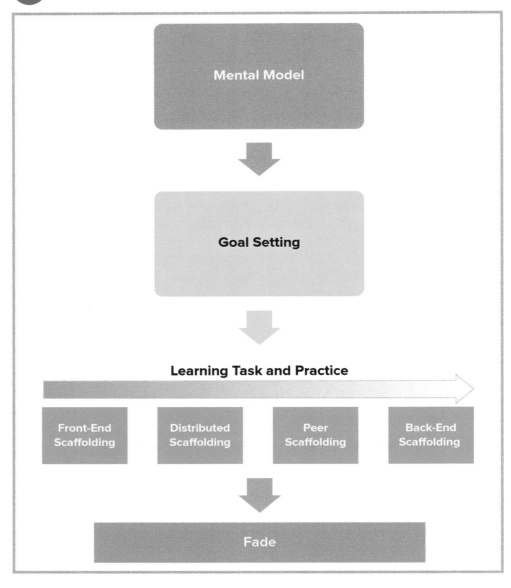

This model incorporates the instructional contingencies contained in Malik's model and the role of effective feedback in these contingencies. Furthermore, this model identifies the direct involvement of each contingency in teacher fading and increased learner responsibility.

Before we further explain, we want to give you a chance to integrate the foundations of scaffolding and the six features of scaffolding (in the box below) into the model on page 36. Place the items below into the model for implementing scaffolding. You may find that some of the foundations and features support multiple parts of the model. For example, making sure the learning is safe is integrated into goal setting, practice, and fading. Adding that to each of those parts of the model is important. Feel free to write them in multiple spots on the model. When you are finished, the model will look quite different than it does now, so mark it up!

FOUNDATIONS OF SCAFFOLDING

- Right-sizing the task

- Making sure learning is a safe experience

- Handling the tricky parts as the student learns

- Providing encouragement, even when there are temporary failures

SIX FEATURES OF SCAFFOLDING

1. **Recruitment.** The first task in scaffolding is to solicit students' interest in the task.

2. **Reduction in degrees of freedom.** This requires that teachers *simplify the task* by reducing the number of acts or steps to reach a solution.

3. **Direction maintenance.** This part of scaffolding is to "*keep them in pursuit of a particular objective*" (Wood et al., p. 98).

4. **Marking critical features.** As part of the support provided, we must highlight the essential features of the task.

5. **Frustration control.** This involves providing some "face-saving" comments for the student who is struggling or offering additional prompts and cues that support success.

6. **Demonstration.** Modeling, thinking aloud, and providing other types of input *allow the student an opportunity to imitate the actions of another*, which may resolve the temporary block in the successful completion of the task.

Let's take a moment and summarize each aspect of the model for *how scaffolding works*. Then, each module after this one will take an in-depth look at the different parts of the model.

Mental models. What are we scaffolding toward? What does proficiency or mastery look like in the end? Mental models are essential to our understanding of complex content, practices, processes, and ideas and represent what we are aiming for or what proficiency and mastery look like for a particular concept, skill, or understanding. For scaffolding to work, we must develop and share a clear representation of what students are working toward in learning. We will take a look at mental models in Module 4.

Goal setting. How much scaffolding is necessary to support learners' progress toward the mental model? How do we scaffold learners as they progress toward proficiency and mastery? Scaffolding works when we identify where students are in their learning journey, make a relative comparison between their current location and the mental model, and set measurable and attainable goals to move forward in their learning. Without goal setting, scaffolding will not be temporary; scaffolding will not work. This is the focus of Module 5.

Learning task and practice. Practice is one of the most important contingencies in scaffolding. Without practice, there is no improvement. However, with certain types of practice, there is no improvement. We have to sort this out. To grow in our learning, promote conceptual development, improve our skills, and enhance our understanding, we must engage in a certain type of practice. Not all practice is the same, and Module 6 will help us compare and contrast the different types of practice, implementing the type that makes scaffolding work.

Front-end, distributed, peer, and back-end scaffolding. Modules 7 through 10 look at different types of scaffolding. These include *front-end scaffolds* that are enacted in advance of the learning. Distributed scaffolds are those that are implemented, monitored, and adjusted during the learning process. Peer scaffolding is when peers learn to support the learning of others. These three scaffolds differ from those that are used *after* the learning tasks have been completed; these are the *back-end scaffolds*.

Fade. Scaffolds are temporary. They are intended to be taken down when the structure underneath is ready. In education, the taking down process is called *fading*, which can occur within a conversation, an activity, a unit, or across the year or course (Martin et al., 2019). Fading involves decreasing the amount or type of scaffolding needed to complete a task or activity. Of course, the goal is for the student to use the skill or concept in a variety of situations, which is known as generalization or transfer. This is the focus of Module 11.

So, there you have it: a model for *how scaffolding works.*

COACH A PEER

Take a few moments and review the Introduction to the playbook. We began our journey with a story about the construction of the 70-story RCA building in New York's Rockefeller Center. We also mentioned that scaffolding for a building has three main components: *standards, ledgers*, and *transoms*.

Here are the definitions of each of these components:

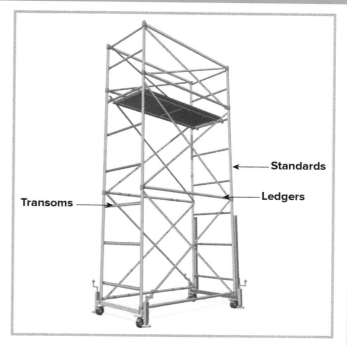

Source: Graphic courtesy of iStock.com/Sussenn

Ledgers are tubes that run horizontally along the length of the scaffold. This component is used to support the working platform of the scaffold. Based on its placement, it determines the height at which the working planks (decks, boards) are staged.

Standards are the perpendicular tubes that transfer the weight load to the baseplates. Standards are connected using pins and socket joints to increase the scaffolding height. Standards are also used to provide stability to the scaffolding and to create working platforms.

Transoms are horizontal tubes that span across ledgers, normally at right angles (90°) to the face of the building. They may also be used to support a working platform. Transoms are an essential part of scaffolding and provide stability and strength to the structure. Without transoms, scaffolding would not be able to support any weight and would collapse. Transoms are generally made of steel or aluminum and are available in various lengths. They are connected to ledgers using clamps or bolts and to each other using couplers. Transoms must be placed at regular intervals along the scaffold length to provide support and stability.

Consider these definitions for the three main components of a scaffold. Teach a peer about the ways in which each of these parts is similar to aspects of our model for *how scaffolding works.* In other words, what parts of our model act as ledgers, standards, and transoms as we scaffold our learners' construction of content, skills, and understandings? If you can explain this to another, you're developing your knowledge of scaffolding.

CONCLUSION

In this module, we presented a model of scaffolding and we noted that practice had to be integrated into scaffolding for the system to work. In other words, we are integrating several bodies of work: scaffolding and deliberate practice. They need each other and too often are separated in ways that prevent students' learning. We see them as integrally linked with one another.

SELF-ASSESSMENT

Before moving forward, consider the success criteria for this module. You will notice these statements have been revised from "We can" statements to "Can I?" questions. Using the traffic light scale, with red being not confident, yellow being somewhat confident, and green indicating very confident, how confident are you in your understanding of the model for how scaffolding works? You'll also want to take note of evidence you have for your self-assessment.

SUCCESS CRITERIA	SELF-ASSESSMENT	EVIDENCE
Can I describe what is meant by contingencies in scaffolding?		
Can I describe a model for implementing scaffolding in our schools and classrooms?		
Can I support our scaffolding model with the research on instructional scaffolding?		

Access resources, tools, and guides
for this module at the companion website:
resources.corwin.com/howscaffoldingworks

4

MENTAL MODELS

LEARNING INTENTION

We are learning about the role of mental models in scaffolding student learning.

SUCCESS CRITERIA

We will know we are successful when

- We can describe what a mental model is and is not.
- We can explain how a mental model helps us to scaffold student learning.
- We can construct and communicate a mental model for an upcoming concept, skill, or understanding.

How do you describe mental models or the explanation of how things work? Use the following question stems to jump-start your thinking.

- What mental models do you have for your job? How do you know what strong performance looks like?

- What mental models do your students need to be successful?

We ended the last module revisiting the fascinating story behind the RCA building, now known as 30 Rockefeller Plaza. While building a skyscraper in a major city no longer captures the same attention as the RCA building in the 1930s, such a feat is still very complex and very difficult. Such a feat requires careful attention to details, processes, and the laws of physics. This is communicated to those building the skyscraper; the individuals who take the vision vertical, so to speak.

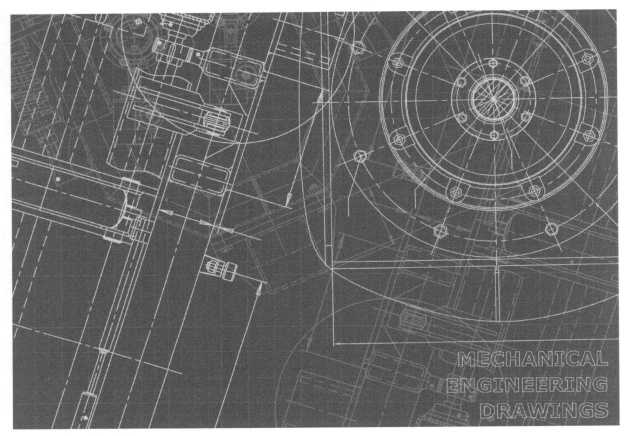

Source: iStock.com/Bubushonok

A blueprint is a two-dimensional drawing that provides the essential details about the construction project. In the 1930s there were blueprints that presented the essential details to the individuals eating their lunch on the beam—the beam that we believed was suspended 69 stories above the ground. Blueprints provide a visual representation of what exactly needs to be built.

Take a moment and think about the information found in a blueprint. List those items here.

-
-
-

Now think about the information that is *not* found in a blueprint but is still found in a building. List those items here.

-

-

-

-

Details such as dimensions, parts, placement, and materials for each construction project are found somewhere on the blueprint and communicated in a way that makes sense to those executing the building project. This provides the essential information needed to complete the project successfully and correctly. Blueprints help construction workers know where to place scaffolds.

In addition to dimensions, blueprints also help communicate the purpose of the project—what this project is seeking to provide or do for the neighborhood, town, city, state, or country (e.g., commercial, residential, industrial). Blueprints also provide other essential information including building codes, installation techniques, measurements, and quality standards.

Revisit your answers to the above prompt. Update your lists based on your new learning. What is not included on a blueprint is just as important as what is included on a blueprint. For example, the type and color of the carpet, the style of furniture, the design of the window treatments or signage, who will be in what room, etc. These are not essential to the construction of the building. Instead, these examples, along with the ones you listed above, are individual and unique choices made by the occupants of the building.

You may already see where we are going with this line of thinking.

✳ Use What You Know

Flip back to the previous module, page 38, and review the summary about mental models. Using the Venn diagram on the next page, compare and contrast mental models and blueprints.

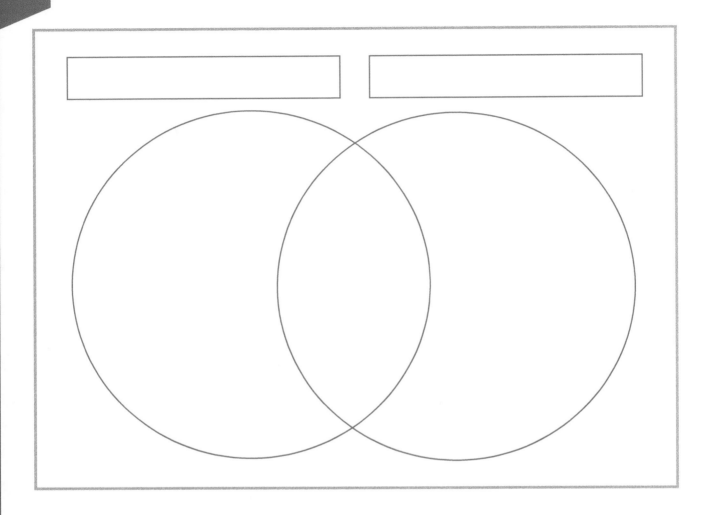

Now let's tie this together.

➡ Mental models are the blueprints for learning.

➡ Just like blueprints, mental models provide the essential information needed to achieve proficiency or mastery in content, skills, and understandings.

➡ What is not included in the mental model communicates where the learner can personalize their learning and make individual choices about aspects of their learning.

➡ Mental models are required for us to decide what scaffolds we may need to support student learning.

DEVELOPING MENTAL MODELS

In *The Success Criteria Playbook* (Almarode et al., 2021) we looked at four examples of complex and often difficult learning:

1. Constructing a viable mathematical argument

2. Gathering compelling scientific evidence

3. Using text features to make meaning

4. Comparing two historical accounts of the same event

We will use these examples here to highlight the connection between clarity for learning and scaffolding. If you are not familiar with the other playbook, that is fine. That will not hinder our learning here. Either way, we want to develop the blueprint, or mental model, for this learning. We must identify and articulate the essential information needed to achieve proficiency or mastery in these areas while at the same time identifying and articulating where the learner can personalize their learning and make individual choices.

In the chart below, we listed the essential information needed to achieve proficiency or mastery in content, skills, and understandings. Remember, even if you do not teach this particular discipline, reviewing this example gets you ready for doing this in your own classroom, with your own learners.

Constructing a viable mathematical argument	Gathering compelling scientific evidence	Using text features to make meaning	Comparing two historical accounts of the same event
• Identify the key aspects of the mathematical problem.	• Describe the scientific question.	• Summarize the information in the text.	• Identify the essential features of the historical event (e.g., people, places, time period).
• Describe the approach or approaches for solving the problem.	• Connect the scientific question to the hypothesis.	• Link that summary to specific evidence from the text.	• Identify and evaluate sources to analyze.
• Explain the argument using mathematics vocabulary.	• Identify the independent and dependent variables.	• Identify the text features included in the text.	• Analyze the sources.
• Present the argument in a logical sequence that connects the previous step, current step, and next step.	• Connect the variables to the data.	• Describe the information presented by the text feature.	• Organize the information provided by the sources.
• Assess the reasonableness of the solution.	• Organize the data in a way that addresses the scientific question.	• Explain how the text feature contributed to understanding the text.	• Compare and contrast the accounts.
• Identify alternative arguments and address them in the explanation.	• Explain the data.	• Relate the evidence from the text, the text features, and the meaning of the text.	• Share the comparison between the accounts.
	• Address alternative hypotheses.		
	• Articulate follow-up questions or areas for investigation.		

COACH A PEER

Talk with a peer to identify an upcoming task or learning experience that is both complex and difficult for learners. This task or learning experience should be a task that will require scaffolding. Whether shading in a still life drawing for art, dribbling in physical education, or analyzing a poem, ask your peer about the essential information needed to achieve proficiency or mastery in content, skills, and understandings. Record them in the chart below. We have left space for you to select multiple tasks, but you can always download copies of this template at the book's companion website.

LEARNING EXPERIENCE OR TASK: _____	LEARNING EXPERIENCE OR TASK: _____	LEARNING EXPERIENCE OR TASK: _____	LEARNING EXPERIENCE OR TASK: _____
•	•	•	•
•	•	•	•
•	•	•	•
•	•	•	•
•	•	•	•
•	•	•	•
•	•	•	•
•	•	•	•
•	•	•	•
•	•	•	•

Remember, *what is not included in our blueprint or mental model is just as important as what is included in the mental model.* These aspects of the mental model represent the individual and unique choices that may be left to the learners. Or, as we will soon see, serve as our starting point for scaffolding the learning experience or task. Return to our four examples and see what was left out of the mental model.

Constructing a viable mathematical argument	Gathering compelling scientific evidence	Using text features to make meaning	Comparing two historical accounts of the same event
• The type of problem • How the argument is presented (e.g., written, verbally) • Whether the learning experience or task is done independently, with a partner, or in a group	• The specific scientific question • The specific way of organizing the data • How the evidence is collected • How the data is explained and alternative hypotheses	• The specific text • The specific strategies used for identifying evidence • How to share the summary and evidence	• The specific historical event • The available sources • The text complexity of the available sources • Ways to organize information • Ways to organize the compare and contrast task • How the analysis is presented

Return to your learning experiences or tasks and think about the essential information NOT included to achieve proficiency or mastery in content, skills, and understandings. Record them in the chart below. Again, we have left space for you to select multiple tasks, but you can always download copies of this template online, at the book's companion website.

Learning Experience or Task: _____	Learning Experience or Task: _____	Learning Experience or Task: _____	Learning Experience or Task: _____
•	•	•	•

What we have essentially done is develop the blueprint for learning. This includes the essential information needed to complete the learning experience or task successfully and correctly. We identified the dimensions, parts, placement, and materials for each learning experience or task. This is the work we do with our PLC+, content-area planning team, or grade-level planning team. These cannot be kept a secret as blueprints are held in secret by the architects who create them. We must communicate these mental models to our learners so that they can take an active role in their learning. Mental models must be communicated in a way that makes sense to those executing the building project or, in schools and classrooms, engaging in the learning experience or task. How do we provide the essential information needed to complete the learning experience or task successfully and correctly? We have to do more than put this on a sheet of paper like a blueprint. That is where we are going next.

COMMUNICATING MENTAL MODELS

Mental models must be communicated to our learners so that they are clear on the critical features of the learning experience or task. What exactly must they know, do, and understand at the level of proficiency and mastery? What is the end result? Where do they get to make decisions about their personalized approach and where are they held accountable for specific aspects of the learning experience or task?

Communicating mental models falls on a continuum and varies between teacher-driven approaches and learner-driven approaches. For example, we might share an exemplar accompanied by a list of look-fors. That approach is teacher centered. A more student-centered approach might involve sharing several examples with learners that include some high-quality examples and some not-so-good examples. *Then, we can facilitate an analysis of those examples and develop a list of the essential information needed to achieve proficiency or mastery in content, skills, and understandings.* We should not be surprised by the fact that we communicate mental models through scaffolding as well—early in the year we may take a more teacher-centered approach and remove the scaffold to offer a more student-centered approach as we build student capacity in developing their own mental models.

Let's develop a plan for communicating mental models. First, consider the examples we provide based on the four learning experiences and tasks we have been working with in this module.

	Constructing a viable mathematical argument	Gathering compelling scientific evidence	Using text features to make meaning	Comparing two historical accounts of the same event
Ideas for communicating a mental model	Prepare a Loom recording modeling the exemplary construction of a mathematical argument; provide a list of look-fors that learners must identify while watching the recording.	Show an example and a non-example; have learners discuss the differences between the two examples; develop a class list of essential characteristics.	Provide several examples using different modalities (e.g., a written example, an EdPuzzle or PlayPosit clip with questions, a visual example); provide a list of look-fors that learners must identify while watching the recording.	Share several examples of varying quality and have learners compare and contrast the examples; develop a class list of essential characteristics.

Okay, your turn. How will you communicate the mental model?

	Learning Experience or Task: _____	Learning Experience or Task: _____	Learning Experience or Task: _____	Learning Experience or Task: _____
Ideas for communicating a mental model				

CONCLUSION

Constructing and communicating mental models are the first steps in scaffolding learning. The power of creating a learning blueprint lies in how that blueprint establishes information such as *dimensions, parts, placement*, and *materials* for the learning experience or task. Essential information must be found in the mental model and communicated to our learners in a way that allows us and them to set goals for their learning progress toward proficiency or mastery. Yes, goal setting is the next part of the model and is derived from the mental model we construct and communicate. That is the focus of our next module.

SELF-ASSESSMENT

Before moving forward, consider the success criteria for this module. You will notice these statements have been revised from "We can" statements to "Can I?" questions. Using the traffic light scale, with red being not confident, yellow being somewhat confident, and green indicating very confident, how confident are you in your understanding of mental models in scaffolding? You'll also want to take note of evidence you have for your self-assessment.

SUCCESS CRITERIA	SELF-ASSESSMENT	EVIDENCE
Can I describe what a mental model is and is not in my classroom?	●━━━━━━━━●	
Can I explain how a mental model helps us to scaffold student learning?	●━━━━━━━━●	
Can I construct and communicate a mental model for an upcoming concept, skill, or understanding?	●━━━━━━━━●	

Access resources, tools, and guides
for this module at the companion website:
resources.corwin.com/howscaffoldingworks

5

GOAL SETTING

How do you describe goal setting in learning contexts? Use the following question stems to jump-start your thinking.

- What is the value of having goals?

- How are goals identified for students?

- How are goals communicated to students?

Scaffolding works when we work collaboratively with our students to leverage the mental models in setting goals in learning. Returning to the topic of our previous module and the metaphor of the blueprint, goal setting is similar to mapping out a plan for which part of the RCA building we are working on today. Let's say that the general contractor takes a look at the blueprint for the building project. They then decide that today, the crew is going to begin running the electricity and plumbing on the thirteenth floor.

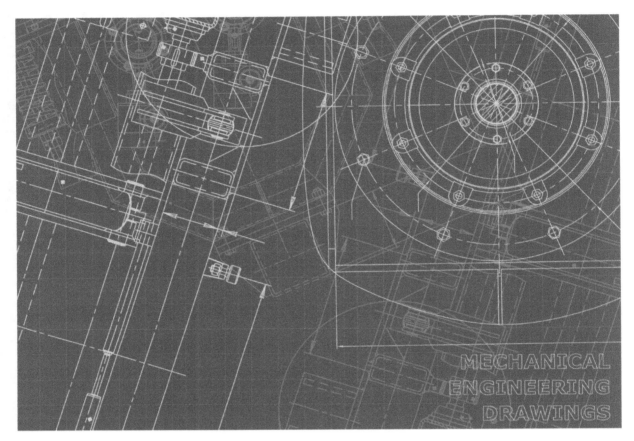

Source: iStock.com/Bubushonok

This goal allows both the general contractor and their colleagues to make key decisions about when scaffolding needs to be placed, what materials and supplies are required, and what codes and regulations will be guiding the work. This is exactly how goal setting plays out in our schools and classrooms; this is how goal setting makes scaffolding work.

PREPARING FOR GOAL SETTING

Once we have constructed and communicated a mental model of the learning experience or task, we must map out a plan for scaffolding learning. Where will we place the scaffolds? How long with the scaffolds stay in place? What will the scaffolds look like? Goal setting zeros in on the specific aspect of the mental model that is the greatest need or top priority for moving learning forward.

How do you know what part of the mental model needs priority over other parts of the mental model?

To know which part of the mental model needs priority or simply where to start with scaffolding we must generate evidence that tells us and our learners where they are in their learning journey. Without evidence generated by initial assessment tasks, we do not have any insight into the strengths and opportunities within the mental model. Plus, we run the risk of over-scaffolding and creating unproductive success, or under-scaffolding and creating unproductive failure. More on this in the next module.

In the chart below, you will see the learning experiences and tasks from the previous module. Only this time, we are going to generate a list of the evidence we need to set goals and place the scaffolding. We will get one started for you and let you practice with the others. Soon after, you will go through this same process with the learning experiences or tasks you selected from your own classroom.

Learning Experience or Task	Features of the Mental Model	Evidence Needed From Initial Assessment Tasks
Constructing a viable mathematical argument	• Identify the key aspects of the mathematical problem. • Describe the approach or approaches for solving the problem. • Explain the argument using mathematics vocabulary. • Present the argument in a logical sequence that connects the previous step, current step, and next step. • Assess the reasonableness of the solution. • Identify alternative arguments and address them in the explanation.	As an initial task several days before the start of this unit, provide learners with several problems to choose from and solve. Then, with their table teams, have them develop a justification for why they selected a particular approach; listen and observe student interactions to identify strengths and opportunities.
Gathering compelling scientific evidence	• Describe the scientific question. • Connect the scientific question to the hypothesis. • Identify the independent and dependent variables. • Connect the variables to the data. • Organize the data in a way that addresses the scientific question. • Explain the data. • Address alternative hypotheses. • Articulate follow-up questions or areas for investigation.	
Using text features to make meaning	• Summarize the information in the text. • Link that summary to specific evidence from the text. • Identify the text features included in the text.	

(Continued)

(Continued)

Learning Experience or Task	Features of the Mental Model	Evidence Needed From Initial Assessment Tasks
Using text features to make meaning (continued)	• Describe the information presented by the text feature. • Explain how the text feature contributed to understanding the text. • Relate the evidence from the text, the text features, and the meaning of the text.	
Comparing two historical accounts of the same event	• Identify the essential features of the historical event (e.g., people, places, time period). • Identify and evaluate sources to analyze. • Analyze the sources. • Organize the information provided by the sources. • Compare and contrast the accounts. • Share the comparison between the accounts.	

Excellent! Now let's start listing the evidence you need for the learning experiences or tasks in your classroom. Flip back to the previous module to review the aspects of the mental model you developed for the learning experiences and tasks. This evidence is absolutely necessary for setting goals and placing the first scaffolds in the learning process. Without this vital part of the process, scaffolding will not work. Again, we have left space for you to select multiple tasks, but you can always download copies of this template at the book's companion website.

 Use What You Know

Learning Experience or Task	Evidence Needed From Initial Assessment Tasks
Learning Experience or Task: _____	
Learning Experience or Task: _____	
Learning Experience or Task: _____	
Learning Experience or Task: _____	

STEPS TO GOAL SETTING

Once we have generated and gathered evidence around the different aspects of the mental model, we must interpret that evidence and translate that interpretation into goals. This process works best when learners are involved in setting their own goals and mapping out a plan for meeting those goals. However, this process must be scaffolded as well. We might first set the goals, then set them collaboratively, and finally, allow learners to set their own goals. Either way, the characteristics of quality goal setting are the same.

1. The **goal we set for our learners or that learners set for themselves must be meaningful and necessary**. The goal should be related to specific opportunities for growth. There is simply no value in setting a goal for something the learner can already do well. This requires us to work alongside our learners and interpret the evidence generated in the initial assessment task. What were the strengths and opportunities uncovered by the evidence?

2. The **goal must be specific, measurable, attainable, and realistic**. Setting goals that are too general can lead to a lack of focus and motivation. For example, a goal of "getting better at math" lacks the specificity needed to develop measurable and attainable steps toward that goal. And, realistically, what does that mean? A goal that a learner "will utilize the multiplication chart to verify their calculation of a common denominator when adding two fractions" is specific, measurable, attainable, and realistic.

3. There must be a **system for documenting the goal** and placing the goal in a conspicuous place. If we set a goal and then never see or look at the goal, that goal will soon be forgotten. By documenting the goal and placing the goal in our interactive notebooks, on our desks, in our literacy folder, or on our student growth chart in the back of the room, the goal is in the visual field and therefore our minds and our students' minds.

4. We must **create a plan for moving toward the goal.** Setting a goal is one thing. Creating a plan is another thing altogether. Just as with the builder's blueprint and plan for running the electricity and plumbing on the thirteenth floor, the plan for learning enables us to identify where the scaffolding happens. Quality goal setting requires that we plan for moving toward that goal. The plans that are most helpful are those that require learners to identify and reflect on their perceived barriers or challenges. This spotlights where to place scaffolds. This also spotlights where we must seek to gradually remove the scaffold and increase learner responsibility.

5. Finally, quality goal setting includes **a system for monitoring progress and check-ins** on progress toward the goal. Whether using teacher-student conferencing or student-student conferences, the monitoring of progress allows us to adjust the level of scaffolding, move the scaffolding to a different location, or completely remove the scaffolding.

> This process works best when learners are involved in setting their own goals and mapping out a plan for meeting those goals.

COACH A PEER

Take a moment and reflect on the five qualities of effective goal setting. Using the space below, explain the connection between the following ideas from the past several modules. What is the relationship between the following?

1. Mental models

2. Evidence

3. Goal setting

4. Scaffolding

5. Fading

6. Increased learner responsibility

To support the process of goal setting, we have provided three templates for you to use. These templates are available online as Word documents so that you can change the headings or specific categories within each template. The language of learning **in your school and classroom** must be consistent across this work as well. However, that language does not have to be the same language I use in my school or classroom. If we call it one thing in our templates, it does not mean you have to call it that same thing in your classroom. Again, just be consistent within your school and classroom.

You may have to scaffold the goal-setting process. You may need to remove some of the parts of these templates and add them later as your learners build capacity toward self-reflection, self-monitoring, and self-assessing.

The language of learning in your school and classroom must be consistent across this work.

Before moving into the next module, take a moment and reflect on your learning. Goal setting aligns with the **foundations of scaffolding** and focuses on the features of scaffolding.

Flip back to the foundations of scaffolding on page 37. In the space provided, write down which of the foundations are highlighted by the construction and communicating mental models.

Flip back to the **features of scaffolding**. Write down which of those features are highlighted by goal setting.

CONCLUSION

We have focused on goal setting as a critical aspect of scaffolding. It's what we scaffold toward. When we have shared goals with students, and students know what success looks like, they are much more likely to allocate resources (time, attention, effort) to learning. And, when students have goals, they are much more likely to integrate the advice you give, in the form of scaffolds that ensure deeper learning.

Goal-Setting Conference

Student Name:
Date:
Description of Initial Task Assessment:

What are your strengths based on the initial assessment?	Where are your opportunities for growth based on the initial assessment?

What are the next steps in your learning?	What are my next steps in supporting your learning?

_____   _____

Student Signature   **Date**

Goal Action Plan

What is my goal?	Why did I select this goal?	How will I hold myself accountable?

What are potential obstacles or barriers to reaching my goal?	What resources will I need to reach my goal?

Here are the steps I am going to take to reach my goal:

Goal Tracking Sheet

Name	Check-In Point							
	1 Date: _____	2 Date: _____	3 Date: _____	4 Date: _____	5 Date: _____	6 Date: _____	7 Date: _____	8 Date: _____

SELF-ASSESSMENT

Before moving forward, consider the success criteria for this module. You will notice these statements have been revised from "We can" statements to "Can I?" questions. Using the traffic light scale, with red being not confident, yellow being somewhat confident, and green indicating very confident, how confident are you in your learning around goal setting and the role it plays in scaffolding? You'll also want to take note of evidence you have for your self-assessment.

SUCCESS CRITERIA	SELF-ASSESSMENT	EVIDENCE
Can I describe the steps in goal setting?		
Can I identify the principles of effective goal setting?		
Can I collaborate with our students to set goals for their learning?		

Access resources, tools, and guides
for this module at the companion website:
resources.corwin.com/howscaffoldingworks

6

DELIBERATE PRACTICE

What is the role of practice in scaffolding? Use the following question stems to jump-start your thinking.

- What types of practice seem to work? What types do not?

- How much practice do students need to develop mastery of a skill or concept?

Return to the previous examples within the playbook. For instance, take a look at Module 1 where we highlighted teaching someone to ride a bike. You also came up with a task or tasks on your own. Did you notice the role that practice played? For the child learning to ride a bike, they had to practice, first with support from another person and then increasingly on their own. The same is probably true with the situation you selected and analyzed. Practice is an important aspect of learning. Practice is necessary for the fading of supports. The role of practice is vital in the model for *how scaffolding works*.

Take a moment and quickly sketch from memory the working model for *how scaffolding works*. After you draw the model, flip back to page 36 in Module 3 to see how you did. Make any edits or revisions to your drawing.

THE ROLE OF PRACTICE

The instructional scaffolds that we provide for our learners are based on the practice that we ask them to do and whether or not they engage in that practice. We recognize that *practice* is not a favored term in some education circles. Practice evokes a wide range of ideas and emotions from mindless handouts, countless repetitive questions or problems, and anxiety over getting the practice done. Furthermore, some practice sessions are graded—not given feedback—negating the idea of the task or exercise being practice. However, there are two things to consider with practice. First, practice makes permanent, not perfect. If a learner engages in practice but practices the "wrong way," that is what he or she will learn—the wrong way. Therefore, we must develop and provide practice opportunities that are scaffolded for our learners. Without sufficient scaffolds, practice opportunities will not move learning forward and prevent us from fading the scaffolding.

Second, not all practice is the same. Let's look at three scenarios.

Scenario 1. Every morning, a group of students gathers in the school's media center to play chess. They rotate who plays whom and simply play every day from the time the first bus drops off students at the school until the bell rings, signaling the start of homeroom.

Scenario 2. Zamari does not just arbitrarily select a chess opponent in the morning. He seeks out individuals that frequently win their chess matches. His goal is to reduce the number of moves to checkmate. So, while playing with an opponent he assesses as being "better at chess," he studies the moves of his opponent and reflects on his performance after each match. He often asks questions during the match to get information about what his opponent was thinking when he or she made a certain move.

Scenario 3. Ava's uncle is a competitive chess player. While not in the top 1,000, her uncle is considered an expert relative to Ava. Ava's uncle will set up different board configurations and analyzes Ava's decisions and moves within those configurations. Her uncle coaches her and teaches her various techniques or approaches to different chessboard configurations.

In the space below, identify the similarities and differences between these three scenarios. What do you notice about these three scenarios?

Similarities	Differences

Just as there were three scenarios above, there are three different types of practices: naive, purposeful, and deliberate (Ericsson & Pool, 2016). In the table below, each of the three types of practice is listed, along with a brief summary of that type of practice. Use the space in the right column to come up with examples from your own experiences for each type of practice.

Type of Practice	Definition	My Examples
Naive practice	Going through the motions; repetition of the task with no goal.	
Purposeful practice	Goal-directed and focused, it includes feedback and is challenging.	
Deliberate practice	In addition to the aspects of purposeful practice, there is defined expertise, and a teacher provides guidance activities.	

Take a moment and return to the three scenarios involving chess players. Label each scenario based on the type of practice (e.g., naive, purposeful, and deliberate) presented in that scenario.

Reflect on all the practice opportunities you offer your learners in your school or classroom. If all those practice opportunities represent 100%, what percentage of those opportunities represent naive practice, purposeful practice, and deliberate practice? Use the space below to visually represent your response. We have provided an example for you.

Our Example:

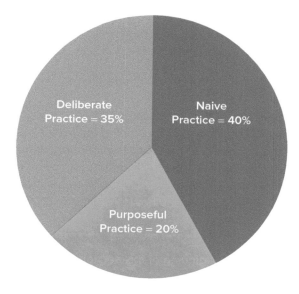

Your Response:

PRACTICE AND SCAFFOLDING

To build the bridge between practice and scaffolding, let's consider the practice of athletes. There are significant differences between you, me, and Serena Williams or Gabby Douglas. As amateurs and casual players, we typically engage in naive practice, perhaps practicing the sport on weekends. While we may enjoy the sport, we are probably not goal focused and rarely have the intent of developing expertise beyond what is required to enjoy the sport. Now consider Horacio, a tenth grader who loves tennis and plans to play in college. He is on the team at his high school as well as a club team that plays at the local recreational center. He has clear goals and is very focused on his skill development in tennis. He has peers video-record him so that he can watch his performance and analyze his decisions and execution of skills to find areas for improvement and improve his skills. In other words, he engages in purposeful practice. In addition, he knows what expert players do and his coaches provide him with specific guidance on the skills he needs to develop. Therefore, they customize his practice to address those skills. In this case, Horacio is engaged in deliberate practice.

As Ericsson and Pool noted,

> We are drawing a clear distinction between purposeful practice—in which a person tries very hard to push himself or herself to improve—and practice that is both purposeful and informed. In particular, deliberate practice is informed and guided by the best performers' accomplishments and by an understanding of what these expert performers do to excel. Deliberate practice is purposeful practice that knows where it is going and how to get there. (2016)

Return to your responses to the questions at the beginning of this section. Those questions were:

- What types of practice seem to work? What types do not?
- How much practice do students need to develop mastery of a skill or concept?

After learning about the three different types of practice, please select a different color or pen or pencil to revise or edit your earlier responses. What would you add to your response? What might need revising based on your new understanding of naive, purposeful, and deliberate practice?

GETTING LEARNERS TO ENGAGE IN DELIBERATE PRACTICE

Deliberate practice is required for teacher fading and increased learner responsibility through scaffolding. There is considerable research on deliberate practice. For example, across three meta-analyses, there are 161 studies, including 13,689 students, resulting in 316 effects (www.visiblelearningmetax.com). Together, the average effect size is 0.79, suggesting that this type of practice has the potential to ramp up student learning.

Unfortunately, students rarely engage in deliberate practice. One of the reasons for the paucity of deliberate practice is that many of the practice opportunities or tasks offered to them only require naive practice (e.g., just keep reading, work more problems, answer more questions, keep taking layups, or as mentioned earlier, keep playing chess). The other reason students rarely engage in deliberate practice is that deliberate practice is challenging. Students may actively try to avoid deliberate practice, opting for the more comfortable, less challenging naive practice. When students simply go through the motions to please their teachers, they will not realize the powerful impact of deliberate practice. As we shall see, having goals, pushing past your comfort zone, responding to feedback, understanding what expertise looks like, and accepting the challenge are all important aspects of deliberate practice; practice that requires scaffolding. So, how do we increase deliberate practice opportunities and motivate learners to engage in those opportunities?

MOTIVATING LEARNERS TO ENGAGE IN DELIBERATE PRACTICE

Take a moment and reflect on practice opportunities, deliberate practice opportunities that were successful. In other words, those deliberate practice opportunities that learners engaged in and benefited from by moving their learning forward. How were these opportunities different from those that were not successful? Jot down your response in the space below.

When looking for research on how to motivate learners to practice, we have to look no further than our school gymnasium. This area of research is well-known in physical education. The work of Block (1995), Hastie et al. (2013), and Tjeerdsma (1995) highlight three essential characteristics of practice tasks that motivate learners to engage in deliberate practice:

1. Success oriented

2. Autonomy supportive

3. Developmentally appropriate

Let's look at these individually.

Success oriented. Learners will struggle to find the motivation to engage in practice—specifically, deliberate practice—if they do not experience success. If our learners never experience success, we certainly cannot expect them to link deliberate practice and moving forward in their learning. We must develop and provide deliberate practice opportunities that allow learners to experience success.

Flip back to Module 4 on page 45. In that module, we identified the essential information needed to achieve proficiency or mastery in content, skills, and understandings. This allowed us to develop a mental model for specific learning experiences or tasks. We also acknowledged aspects that were NOT included in the mental model. First, review your examples of those aspects NOT included in the mental model. We have provided our examples to get you started.

Constructing a viable mathematical argument	Gathering compelling scientific evidence	Using text features to make meaning	Comparing two historical accounts of the same event
• The type of problem • How the argument is presented (e.g., written, verbally) • Whether the learning experience or task is done independently, with a partner, or in a group	• The specific scientific question • The specific way of organizing the data • How the evidence is collected • How the data is explained and alternative hypotheses	• The specific text • The specific strategies used for identifying evidence • How to share the summary and evidence	• The specific historical event • The available sources • The text complexity of the available sources • Ways to organize information • Ways to organize the compare and contrast task • How the analysis is presented

As you have heard before, what is not included in our blueprint or mental model is just as important as what is included in the mental model. Not only do these aspects of the mental model represent the individual and unique choices that may be left to the learners, but they also represent areas we can modify or adapt to increase success rates within the deliberate practice opportunity.

The following chart shows our four learning experiences or tasks and how we can use the items not included in the blueprint or model to offer a great opportunity for learners to experience success. See if you can brainstorm ideas for increasing experiences of success during deliberate practice sessions. We modeled one for you.

Use What You Know

	Ways to Increase Opportunities for Success During Deliberate Practice Sessions
Constructing a viable mathematical argument	• Varying the type of problem allows me to adjust the numbers or text of the problem so that learners can successfully solve the problem and focus more on practicing how to construct the argument; prevents the difficulty of the problem from reducing motivation. • Offering learners different ways to present the argument allows them to focus more on articulating the argument and not on the modality; prevents the presentation of the argument from reducing motivation. • Working collaboratively allows for peer-to-peer scaffolding; the social interaction may increase motivation.
Gathering compelling scientific evidence	
Using text features to make meaning	
Comparing two historical accounts of the same event	

Now it is your turn. Revisit your learning experiences and tasks on page 54. How could those features not included in our blueprint or mental model be used to increase success? Use the template below to record your thinking.

	Ways to Increase Opportunities for Success During Deliberate Practice Sessions
Learning Experience or Task: _____	
Learning Experience or Task: _____	
Learning Experience or Task: _____	
Learning Experience or Task: _____	

Autonomy supportive. Deliberate practice opportunities should seek to build learners' sense of ownership in their learning. Learners will be more motivated to engage in deliberate practice if they

➡ Have a variety of tasks to choose from

➡ Are able to personalize their practice sessions

➡ Receive feedback during and after the session

➡ Have ways to measure their own personal growth

➡ Are allowed to take risks and try out more difficult tasks

➡ Work with peers

Returning to our four learning experiences or tasks, let's brainstorm ideas for offering autonomy to learners. As before, we modeled one for you.

	Ways to Offer Autonomy to Learners
Constructing a viable mathematical argument	
Gathering compelling scientific evidence	• Learners are offered several options of scientific phenomena for generating, gathering, and interpreting evidence. • Learners get to decide how to present their data (e.g., computer, poster paper). • Learners can use Loom, Flipgrid, or another technology to present their compelling scientific evidence.
Using text features to make meaning	
Comparing two historical accounts of the same event	

Alright, now you try this out with your learning experiences or tasks. Again, revisit your learning experiences and tasks on page 54. How could those features not included in our blueprint or mental model be used to support learner autonomy? Use the template on the next page to record your thinking.

	Ways to Offer Autonomy to Learners
Learning Experience or Task: _____	
Learning Experience or Task: _____	
Learning Experience or Task: _____	
Learning Experience or Task: _____	

Developmentally appropriate. The final essential characteristic is *developmental appropriateness*. If we adjust the type of problem from which learners construct an argument, give them choices about scientific phenomena, offer them a variety of texts, or allow them to select a historical event, each one of these approaches must still be developmentally appropriate. The mathematics problem must not require mathematics too difficult. The scientific phenomenon must be safe for the specific age of the learners. The rigor of the text must be aligned with the learners' reading level. The historical event must be appropriate for the learners (e.g., the Holocaust may not be appropriate for second graders, but appropriate for high school learners).

The following chart shows our four learning experiences or tasks and how we can use the items not included in the blueprint or model to offer a great opportunity for learners to experience success. See if you can brainstorm ideas for increasing experiences of success during deliberate practice sessions by ensuring those sessions are developmentally appropriate. We modeled one for you.

	Ways to Ensure Developmental Appropriateness
Constructing a viable mathematical argument	
Gathering compelling scientific evidence	
Using text features to make meaning	<ul><li>Ensure the rigor of the text is appropriate for the learner's current reading level.</li><li>Ensure the learner knows the strategies for active reading and can apply them to the text.</li><li>Ensure the expectations for the presentation are reasonable for the age and grade level of the learner.</li></ul>
Comparing two historical accounts of the same event	

One final time, here is an opportunity for you to try this out with your learning experiences or tasks. Again, revisit your learning experiences and tasks on page 54. How could those features not included in our blueprint or mental model be adjusted for developmental appropriateness? Use the template below to record your thinking.

 Use What You Know

	Ways to Ensure Developmental Appropriateness
Learning Experience or Task: _____	
Learning Experience or Task: _____	
Learning Experience or Task: _____	
Learning Experience or Task: _____	

Deliberate practice results in the most learning. Yet deliberate practice—practice that focuses on areas needing improvement—increases the chances that we will *not* be successful in the beginning. As we adjust the scaffolds—moving scaffolds, increasing scaffolds, removing scaffolds—learners may experience a mixture of success and failure. But not all failure is bad and not all success is good. Depending on the type of failure and success, we make new or different adjustments to the tasks to increase success, autonomy, and developmental appropriateness.

Not all failure is bad and not all success is good.

Just like scaffolding on the RCA building, constant adjustments will be necessary based on learner failure and success. How do failure and success play out in deliberate practice and scaffolding?

PRODUCTIVE FAILURE AND SUCCESS

In reality, as we will see in a later module, we aim to provide students with both purposeful and deliberate practice and eliminate naive practice. When students are engaged in these types of practice, scaffolding keeps students in the game, so to speak. If the practice is too challenging and unscaffolded, we are essentially sending a first-time bike rider out onto the freeway without training wheels. Scaffolding is designed to provide students with productive success and productive failure experiences (Kapur, 2016). Below, find a description of four possible learning events on the left. Connect each one with their conditions on the right. Yes, this is a matching task.

A. *Unproductive failure*   _____ Unguided problem solving

B. *Unproductive success*   _____ Structured problem solving

C. *Productive failure*   _____ Using prior knowledge to figure out a solution followed by more instruction

D. *Productive success*   _____ Memorizing an algorithm without understanding why

Of the four conditions, *unproductive failure* yields the smallest gains, as students' thinking is not guided in any way. Learners are just expected to discover what they should be learning. *Unproductive success* is also of limited value, as individuals in this condition rely on memorization only but don't ever get to why and how this is applied (think of the baby bird that has everything intellectually chewed up for it). There's just no transfer of knowledge. Return to the above matching task and make sure you have made these connections.

Now let's move to the beneficial conditions: *productive failure* and *productive success*. Kapur (2016) explains that

> the difference between productive failure and productive success is a subtle but important one. The goal for productive failure is a preparation for learning from subsequent instruction. Thus, it does not matter if students do not achieve successful problem-solving performance initially. In contrast, the goal for productive success is to learn through a successful problem-solving activity itself. (p. 293)

Effective scaffolding requires a mixture of productive failure and productive success.

Based on Kapur's model, we identified four possible learning events and their impact (see Figure 6.1). Effective scaffolding requires a mixture of productive failure and productive success. We use productive failure to expose a problem the student didn't know existed, and then to follow it with support. Kapur (2019) suggests that "the first job of a teacher isn't to teach. The first job of a teacher is to prepare your students to see, and then to show them."

6.1 FOUR POSSIBLE LEARNING EVENTS

	Unproductive Failure	Unproductive Success	Productive Success	Productive Failure
Type of Learning Event	Unguided problem solving without further instruction	Rote memorization without conceptual understanding	Guided problem solving using prior knowledge and tasks planned for success	Unsuccessful or suboptimal problem solving using prior knowledge, followed by further instruction
Learning Outcome	Frustration that leads to abandoning learning	Completion of the task without understanding its purpose or relevance	Consolidation of learning through scaffolded practice	Learning from errors and ensuring learners persist in generating and exploring representations and solutions
Useful for . . .			Surface learning of new knowledge firmly anchored to prior knowledge	Deep learning and transfer of knowledge
Undermines . . .	Agency and motivation	Goal setting and willingness to seek challenge		
Promotes . . .			Skill development and concept attainment	Use of cognitive, metacognitive, and affective strategies

Source: Frey et al. (2018).

COACH A PEER

Visit the classroom of a peer. Identify tasks that seem to fit into each of the four categories that Kapur identified regarding success and failure. Provide some explanation as to why you classified the task the way that you did. Discuss these with your peer and identify which of these tasks might be most effective in facilitating learning.

UNPRODUCTIVE FAILURE	PRODUCTIVE FAILURE

UNPRODUCTIVE SUCCESS	PRODUCTIVE SUCCESS

CONCLUSION

Deliberate practice provides students with opportunities to experience success and failure, both of which are useful in learning. It's when students are engaged in practice that we can apply scaffolds. We also focused on specific aspects of deliberate practice that need careful consideration if the work that we ask students to do is going to be meaningful. These include a success orientation, supportive of autonomy, and developmentally appropriate.

SELF-ASSESSMENT

Before moving forward, consider the success criteria for this module. You will notice these statements have been revised from "We can" statements to "Can I?" questions. Using the traffic light scale, with red being not confident, yellow being somewhat confident, and green indicating very confident, how confident are you in your learning about deliberate practice? You'll also want to take note of evidence you have for your self-assessment.

SUCCESS CRITERIA	SELF-ASSESSMENT	EVIDENCE
Can I compare and contrast the different types of practice?		
Can I explain the differences between productive and unproductive success and failure?		
Can I describe the three characteristics of effective deliberate practice experiences?		
Can I use different techniques to motivate learners to engage in deliberate practice?		

Access resources, tools, and guides
for this module at the companion website:
resources.corwin.com/howscaffoldingworks

7

FRONT-END SCAFFOLDS

LEARNING INTENTION

We are learning about techniques for designing and delivering meaningful front-end scaffolds so that we can bridge gaps and increase access.

SUCCESS CRITERIA

We will know we are successful when

- We can define the meaning and purposes of front-end scaffolds.
- We can identify common errors that occur when using front-end scaffolds.
- We can apply principles of universal design for learning to reduce the need for some front-end scaffolds.
- We can judiciously select and deliver vocabulary front-end scaffolds for texts.

How do you describe front-end scaffolds? Use the following question stems to jump-start your thinking.

- Why would we want or need to front-end some scaffolds?

- When do you think front-end scaffolding is appropriate? When is it not appropriate?

Let's return to the construction metaphor we have used periodically in this playbook, this time considering how the site is initially prepared. One important phase of site preparation is soil testing. This is performed to determine the conditions present before pouring the foundation. Two determinations have to do with water absorption and soil-bearing capacity. It's not enough to have good concrete and footings. How will the soil respond to the laying of the foundation?

Responsive teachers follow a similar process (although they probably aren't wearing the cool yellow safety helmet). They know that it isn't sufficient to have a solid curriculum. How will the students respond to the teaching? Can they absorb what is being taught? Do they have the knowledge-bearing capacity? Like site preparers, they analyze their students in advance to make the necessary adjustments.

FRONT-END SCAFFOLDS

Front-end scaffolds are the methods used in advance of instruction so that students are prepared for the learning to come.

Front-end scaffolds are the methods used in advance of instruction so that students are prepared for the learning to come. These decisions are drawn from a variety of sources, including initial assessments of prerequisite skills and background knowledge. For some students with disabilities, front-end scaffolds, called accommodations in individualized education programs (IEPs) and 504 plans, may be more formally identified. In other cases, front-end scaffolds are designated as part of the linguistic supports designed to benefit multilingual learners. In all cases, the scaffolds are temporary and designed to be faded in the coming weeks or months. Scaffolds, including ones delivered at the front of the lesson, are not the same as modifications, which are long-lasting and fundamentally change what it is the student is learning (see Figure 7.1).

7.1 COMPARING SCAFFOLDS AND MODIFICATIONS

Front-End Scaffolds	Curricular Modifications
Are temporary and used only until they are no longer needed	Are long-term and fixed
Are informed by grade or course standards	Change the grade-level or course goals at the standards level
Designed to bridge to more complex texts and tasks	Tailored to meet the needs of the individual
Determined by the teacher	Determined by the IEP team

Scaffolds developed in advance of the lesson often perform three of the six functions Wood et al. (1976) outlined: *recruitment, reduction in degrees in freedom,* and *marking critical features*. Some front-end scaffolds focus on understanding current skills and knowledge, in an effort to bring the student into the learning. Other techniques, such as chunking a reading into smaller passages, are meant to simplify the task.

One well-known example of front-end scaffolding, reciprocal teaching, does just that (Palincsar & Brown, 1986). Four readers work collaboratively with a longer piece of text that has been segmented in advance by the teacher. That's the front-end scaffold. At the end of each segment, students generate and discuss questions to clarify meaning, summarize, and make predictions about the passage, before moving forward to the next section of the text. Other front-end scaffolds mark critical features through methods such as using graphic organizers or realia for multilingual learners.

One example of a front-end scaffold you have experienced several times is the feature at the beginning of each module listing the learning intentions and success criteria. These statements provide a toehold for what is to come and offer a means for the learner to monitor progress toward goals. These front-end scaffolds hold the potential to accelerate learning of students.

The Visible Learning® database, developed by John Hattie, identifies learning intentions as having an effect size of 0.51, well above the average effect size of 0.40. Success criteria, which are the means by which a project will be judged, have an even stronger potential, at 0.88 (www.visiblelearningmetax.com). While the practice of establishing learning intentions and success criteria should be an ongoing feature of a sound instructional plan, they are temporary in the sense that they change from one lesson to the next (Almarode et al., 2021).

FRONT-END LITERACY SCAFFOLDS

EL Education, a collaboration that began as a partnership between Harvard Graduate School of Education and Outward-Bound USA, describes literacy-focused front-end scaffolds as actions for understanding complex texts before students read them (EL Education, n.d.). They provide these helpful examples:

1. Using learning targets to help students understand the purpose of the reading.

2. Providing visual cues to help students understand targets.

3. Identifying, bolding, and writing in the margins to define words that cannot be understood through the context of the text.

4. Chunking long readings into short passages (literally distributing sections on index cards, for example), so that students see only the section they need to tackle.

5. Reading the passage aloud before students read independently.

6. Providing an audio or video recording of a teacher read-aloud that students can access when needed.

7. Supplying a reading calendar at the beginning of longer-term reading assignments, so that teachers in support roles and families can plan for pacing.

8. Pre-highlighting text for some learners so that when they reread independently, they can focus on the essential information.

9. Eliminating the need for students to copy information—and if something is needed (such as a definition of vocabulary), providing it on the handout or other student materials.

Which of these front-end literacy scaffolds do you use most commonly?

USE FRONT-END SCAFFOLDS JUDICIOUSLY

Front-end scaffolds are especially ripe for overuse, which can then have the unintended consequence of reducing opportunities for productive success as well as productive struggle. Well-meaning teachers may commit two common errors in doing so:

→ Over-scaffolding for the entire group, when in fact it was only necessary for a smaller number of students.

→ Frontloading too much vocabulary for a reading, thus exceeding the cognitive load of the students.

✳ Use What You Know

Revisit "Productive Failure and Success," beginning on page 77, to extend your thinking.

How might over-scaffolding undermine productive success?

_____

_____

_____

How might too much frontloaded vocabulary contribute to productive failure?

_____

_____

_____

Avoiding the error of unnecessary front-end scaffolds. Scaffolds are tools to address immediate learning needs. However, as with all things related to learning, those needs vary across the group. In a stunning study ingeniously titled *The Hidden Lives of Learners*, Nuthall (2007) had students respond in real time as to whether what the instructor was teaching in that moment was something new or something known. He learned that about 40% of the time, students already knew what was being taught. Now, of course, content should not be relentlessly and unflinchingly new at every moment. In fact, it is an axiom of education that we continually are moving from the known to the new. But 40% is a pretty startling figure. Here's the rub: it's not the same 40% for all students. Needs diverge, and some students know *x* while others know *y*.

Figuring out those varying needs requires some initial assessments, and they don't need to be incredibly involved and prolonged. As one example, a geometry teacher might administer an anticipation guide at the beginning of a unit on triangles and similarity (see Figure 7.2). This technique is useful for several reasons. First, the before-and-after nature of the anticipation guide provides students with an opportunity to reflect on their learning. Second, and pertinent to this discussion of front-end scaffolds, it provides the teacher with a sense of who has some prior knowledge about the content and who doesn't. Armed with that knowledge, the teacher can provide those students with a small group pre-teaching lesson to build requisite skills.

> **Front-end scaffolds are especially ripe for overuse, which can result in fewer opportunities for productive success and productive struggle.**

 7.2 GEOMETRY ANTICIPATION GUIDE FOR TRIANGLE SIMILARITY

Directions: Read each statement and mark **T** if the statement is true and **F** if the statement is false. Be prepared to explain your reasoning.

Before		Statements	After	
True	False		True	False
		The hypotenuse of a right triangle is always the longest side.		
		In the Pythagorean Theorem, the hypotenuse can be labeled either *a*, *b*, or *c*.		
		The vertex of the legs of a right triangle measure 90°.		
		The shortest leg of a right triangle must be labeled *a*.		
		$a^2 + b^2 = c^2$		

Avoiding the error of exceeding cognitive load. It is not uncommon for teachers to frontload vocabulary for their students in advance of reading a complex text. This is typically accomplished by introducing definitions of unfamiliar words and phrases before reading. There's some evidence that frontloading vocabulary can be useful for multilingual learners (Lesaux et al., 2014) and those who are not yet reading at expected levels (August et al., 2009). In fact, we'll return to techniques for pre-teaching vocabulary later in this module.

But let's not forget about the cognitive load of learners. We've witnessed too many lessons where the teacher attempted to frontload a dozen or more vocabulary terms! In all likelihood, so many unfamiliar words and phrases overwhelmed students' working memory (in previous decades this was called short-term memory). The general consensus is that we can hold about five to nine items in our working memory at a given time. Now add to this the complex task of reading and its additional taxing of working memory. A reader has to juggle their knowledge of decoding and syntax, as well as the background knowledge and vocabulary, in order to make sense of the text. Now add too many unfamiliar terms introduced all at once. The result can be a cognitive overload for the learner (Sweller, 1988). In other words, the brain has a finite number of things it can do all at once. We need to be selective in what we are asking those brains to do.

THE HIDDEN LIFE OF YOUR OWN LEARNING

All of us have been on the receiving end of these two errors—unnecessary scaffolding or cognitive overload—in our own learning lives. Recall a time when those have happened to you. What was the situation? What was the effect on you? How would you advise the teacher or instructor to strengthen their teaching?

Situation	What was the effect for you?	What humane and growth-producing advice would you offer now?
You experienced unnecessary front-end scaffolding.		
You experienced cognitive overload.		

UNIVERSAL DESIGN FOR LEARNING

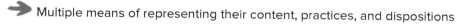

Universal design for learning (UDL) is a set of guiding principles for curriculum development and instruction that can reduce the need for unnecessary scaffolding and modifications. These three principles presume that because learners vary, so do their needs in terms of how they represent, express, and engage in learning (CAST, 2018):

➡ Multiple means of representing their content, practices, and dispositions

➡ Multiple ways of expressing their learning

➡ Multiple forms of engaging in the learning

These assumptions are themselves a kind of front-end scaffold, in the sense that they require planning for variability in advance, rather than retrofitting instructional techniques. The result is that there is a more efficient use of the teacher's time, as well as the students'. We'll use a historical comparison to illustrate what we mean. When the Americans with Disabilities Act (ADA) was passed in 1990, many architectural features of existing buildings had to be retrofitted. Curb cuts, wider doorways to accommodate wheelchairs, and emergency instructions for people who are blind or deaf had to be installed. But the provisions of the ADA that govern architectural design mean that new structures are designed with these features already in place, at a far lower cost than those that had to be retrofitted. The UDL principles of curricular and instructional design work similarly, as these considerations govern design, rather than require numerous retrofitted fixes. As one feature, textbook adoptions require alternative Braille versions for students who are blind, and closed captioning is routinely used to support students with language.

Many of the cells in Figure 7.3 have implications for reducing the need for front-end scaffolds:

➡ **Multiple means of engagement:** Use learning intentions and success criteria to establish goals; highlight the relevance of the topic to be taught to activate background knowledge; reduce distractions.

➡ **Multiple means of representation:** Choose materials that are accessible (closed captioning of videos, Braille versions of print materials, readings that are scaled for a span of reading levels); choose texts that offer footnotes, glossaries, and other text features that guide the reader.

➡ **Multiple meanings of action and expression:** Consider ways students will respond, including universal response opportunities; create structures so that students can organize the concepts they will be learning.

7.3 UNIVERSAL DESIGN FOR LEARNING GUIDELINES

The Universal Design for Learning Guidelines

CAST | Until learning has no limits

Provide multiple means of **Engagement**	Provide multiple means of **Representation**	Provide multiple means of **Action & Expression**
Affective Networks The "WHY" of Learning	Recognition Networks The "WHAT" of Learning	Strategic Networks The "HOW" of Learning

Access

Provide options for **Recruiting Interest** (7)
- Optimize individual choice and autonomy (7.1)
- Optimize relevance, value, and authenticity (7.2)
- Minimize threats and distractions (7.3)

Provide options for **Perception** (1)
- Offer ways of customizing the display of information (1.1)
- Offer alternatives for auditory information (1.2)
- Offer alternatives for visual information (1.3)

Provide options for **Physical Action** (4)
- Vary the methods for response and navigation (4.1)
- Optimize access to tools and assistive technologies (4.2)

Build

Provide options for **Sustaining Effort & Persistence** (8)
- Heighten salience of goals and objectives (8.1)
- Vary demands and resources to optimize challenge (8.2)
- Foster collaboration and community (8.3)
- Increase mastery-oriented feedback (8.4)

Provide options for **Language & Symbols** (2)
- Clarify vocabulary and symbols (2.1)
- Clarify syntax and structure (2.2)
- Support decoding of text, mathematical notation, and symbols (2.3)
- Promote understanding across languages (2.4)
- Illustrate through multiple media (2.5)

Provide options for **Expression & Communication** (5)
- Use multiple media for communication (5.1)
- Use multiple tools for construction and composition (5.2)
- Build fluencies with graduated levels of support for practice and performance (5.3)

Internalize

Provide options for **Self Regulation** (9)
- Promote expectations and beliefs that optimize motivation (9.1)
- Facilitate personal coping skills and strategies (9.2)
- Develop self-assessment and reflection (9.3)

Provide options for **Comprehension** (3)
- Activate or supply background knowledge (3.1)
- Highlight patterns, critical features, big ideas, and relationships (3.2)
- Guide information processing and visualization (3.3)
- Maximize transfer and generalization (3.4)

Provide options for **Executive Functions** (6)
- Guide appropriate goal-setting (6.1)
- Support planning and strategy development (6.2)
- Facilitate managing information and resources (6.3)
- Enhance capacity for monitoring progress (6.4)

Goal

Expert learners who are...

Purposeful & Motivated	Resourceful & Knowledgeable	Strategic & Goal-Directed

Source: CAST (2018).

✳ Use What You Know

If you want to learn more about UDL, spend some time with the interactive version of this chart at http://udlguidelines.cast.org. You can click on each item listed in the cells to learn more about the topic. Choose one item from each of the three principles. What additional suggestions do you see for front-end scaffolds?

My Ideas for Multiple Means of Engagement	My Ideas for Multiple Means of Representation	My Ideas for Multiple Means of Action and Expression

SELECTING FRONT-END VOCABULARY SCAFFOLDS

The purpose of strategically frontloading vocabulary in advance of a reading is to bridge potential barriers that would otherwise significantly interfere with a student's understanding. Notice two important words in that last sentence: *strategically* and *significantly*. By *strategic*, we mean choosing words and phrases that can't be determined otherwise through context clues or the structural characteristics of the word. Take the word *galaxy* as an example. The word defies structural analysis; you can't break it into smaller morphemes to determine its meaning. But it's possible that *galaxy* in a reading about the solar system could be paired with context clues such as a definition and example. *Astronomy* is a term that might be unlocked through structural analysis, as *astro-* refers to stars and *-nomy* indicates it is the study of something. But if the structural analysis skills are beyond the current knowledge levels of the students reading about galaxies, it might be a candidate for a front-end scaffold.

Buehl (2017) notes that "frontloading focuses on assumed knowledge—what an author expects readers to know—that can derail comprehension if it's not acquired" (p. 65). That brings us to the second term: *significantly*. Just because it's a potentially unknown term doesn't mean that it rises to the level of significance for the reading. The word *tunic* appears once in the first chapter of *The Giver* (Lowry, 1993). In the context of the story, it isn't significant (although knowing the meaning of *tunic* might be more significant in a passage about clothing in ancient Greece).

TECHNIQUES FOR FRONT-END VOCABULARY SCAFFOLDS

Without question, vocabulary should be *anchored by text*; teaching vocabulary in isolation as an exercise in memorization of a list of unrelated terms is going to result, at best, in unproductive success. When you have selected the candidates for frontloading, analyze them to see if there are connections you can make regarding *morphology,* such as roots and affixes, or *cognates*, which are especially useful for multilingual learners. For instance, *razonable* in Spanish has a close English cognate: *reasonable.*

Dutro and Moran (2003) describe language through the metaphor of bricks and mortar. While vocabulary words and phrases comprise the bricks of language, they are held together by the mortar, which is to say the academic language used to construct sentences. *Because* and *compare* are two examples of mortar words. When frontloading vocabulary, highlight how the word is used in the context of the reading by pointing out the sentence it appears in and providing another example of how it is used verbally. Further expand students' knowledge by offering *word forms*, as needed. For instance, when frontloading *decision*, you may want to include other word forms such as *decide* and *decisive.*

Other techniques when frontloading vocabulary make the most of visual information. Use *visual cues* such as a graphic organizer or guided notes to further anchor the initial instruction about the terms. These can be in the form of a guide for a reading, such as one used to frontload vocabulary before an introductory reading for eighth graders on the U.S. Constitution. The teacher introduced key vocabulary before the reading, highlighting where the terms would appear in the passage, and using the terms in original sentences. Students used the guided notes to enter the terms (*amendment, constitution, legislative, posterity*, and *tranquility*) next to their corresponding definitions (see Figure 7.4). Another visual technique is the use of realia, photographs, or illustrations to further their initial understanding. These are especially useful when introducing nouns.

7.4   GUIDED NOTES FOR U.S. CONSTITUTION READING

_____ A statement that is added to a document

_____ The act of forming or establishing an organization

_____ Related to a lawmaking assembly

_____ All generations in the future

_____ Being free of worries or disturbances

Finally, multimedia plays a prominent role in classrooms. The use of *computer-assisted instruction* such as a slide presentation to further organize terms, as well as short videos that capitalize on auditory and visual channels of learning, can be useful in front-loading information and terms. For instance, a short video on how volcanoes erupt can help to build initial understanding in advance of the reading about the topic they will be using. Figure 7.5 is a summary of the techniques discussed in this section.

Having said that, it's important to emphasize that too much time spent on frontloading vocabulary means less time for the actual lesson. Frontloading should be limited to essential concepts that are necessary for the text or task to make sense. As we will see in the next module, distributed scaffolds can also be used to address unknown terminology.

 7.5 **10 WAYS TO FRONTLOAD VOCABULARY**

Technique	Explanation	Implementation
Anchor texts	Using academic reading to base activities that allow students to speak, listen, read, and write	• Read aloud and explain mortar words using anchor text • Have students listen to and repeat pronunciation • Practice reading phonemes and syllables • Have students use text as a model for written and read practice
Cognates	Explicitly teaching cognates and false cognates in academic vocabulary	• Use anchor text to show cognates and false cognates • Create a list and what the words would be in the first language • Encourage reading and writing in the first language using cognates
Mortar words	Explicitly teaching brick (or content-specific) words and mortar (or general academic) terms as it relates to content	• Explain the difference between brick and mortar vocabulary • Have students create lists of both • Examine anchor texts for both • Use visuals to support retention
Word forms	Providing vocabulary extension by exploring different forms of the word	• Look for cross-curricular mortar words in anchor text (e.g., factor, subject, synthesize) • Have students create lists of word forms • Practice using words in sentences across content areas

(Continued)

(Continued)

Technique	Explanation	Implementation
Morphology	Teaching the meaning of common root words, prefixes, and suffixes	• Use anchor texts to examine the root words and morphemes in brick and mortar vocabulary • Find other words that share the same root words, prefixes, and suffixes
Computer-assisted instruction	Using presentation software and programs, such as PowerPoint and Prezi	• Show information about cognates, brick and mortar words, different word forms, and morphemes using attractive formats, media clips, hyperlinks, and even narration of text
Content acquisition podcasts	Using short multimedia vignettes	• Create content-based podcasts to help students learn new vocabulary words using images with audio messages • Be selective about morphemes and choose a few text-based academic concepts
Guided visual vocabulary practice	Using flashcards and guided vocabulary practice in the first language	• Solicit four English nouns from students on an academic theme • Develop flashcards in both languages by using visual, auditory, verbal, and motor sensorial skills • Support the vocabulary development of native Spanish speakers
Visual cues	Using graphic organizers to support a student's self-regulation and metacognition	• Use word lists, word cards, graphic organizers, and self-regulation sheets with cooperative learning, explicit instruction, and self-regulation procedures
Promoting adolescent comprehension through text	Activating oral and written language production through new content activities	• Teach five key vocabulary words from an anchor text • Use academic vocabulary in oral and written responses • Facilitate academic discussions and written activities • Use a student-centered approach with collaborative groups • Emphasize oral language production • Revisit and clarify vocabulary words taught in text and throughout each activity

Source: Cuba (2020).

COACH A PEER

Middle school science teacher Ingrid Offenbach is excited about the new unit of instruction she's designed for her students on human organ systems. "I'm going to start with sight and the functions of the human eye," she tells you. Ms. Offenbach plans to introduce the unit next week to her students and then move into a reading about the eye. You notice that the reading is a long one—three pages in length—and includes 16 vocabulary terms she has identified from the reading. She doesn't seem to have a plan for establishing relevance or activating and building background knowledge. What advice do you have for her? Use the chart below to organize your own thinking.

PRINCIPLES AND PRACTICE	ADVICE FOR THE TEACHER
UDL: Multiple means of engagement	
UDL: Multiple means of representation	
UDL: multiple means of action and expression	
Cognitive load	
Identifying prior knowledge	
Establishing goals	
Establishing relevance	
Using vocabulary	
Accessing the text	

CONCLUSION

Front-end scaffolds are those that occur in advance of accessing content and texts. However, lack of knowledge about the needs of students can result in needless over-scaffolding for some students and cognitive overload for others. The sweet spot that we strive for is moving back and forth between productive success and productive struggle, or as John Hattie says, "not too hard, not too boring." Universal design for learning is an important first step in reducing the overall need for scaffolds, including front-end ones. UDL does not replace the need for scaffolds; rather, it can mitigate barrier removal. Commonly used front-end scaffolds are typically related to concepts and texts.

SELF-ASSESSMENT

Before moving forward, consider the success criteria for this module. You will notice these statements have been revised from "We can" statements to "Can I?" questions. Using the traffic light scale, with red being not confident, yellow being somewhat confident, and green indicating very confident, how confident are you in your ability to utilize knowledge of front-end scaffolds? You'll also want to take note of evidence you have for your self-assessment.

SUCCESS CRITERIA	SELF-ASSESSMENT	EVIDENCE
Can I define the meaning and purposes of front-end scaffolds?		
Can I identify common errors that occur when using front-end scaffolds?		
Can I apply principles of universal design for learning to reduce the need for some front-end scaffolds?		
Can I judiciously select and deliver vocabulary front-end scaffolds for texts?		

Access resources, tools, and guides
for this module at the companion website:
resources.corwin.com/howscaffoldingworks

8

DISTRIBUTED SCAFFOLDS

LEARNING INTENTION

LEARNING INTENTION

We are learning about techniques for designing and delivering meaningful distributed scaffolds so that we can support learners as they engage in tasks.

SUCCESS CRITERIA

We will know we are successful when

- We can define the meaning and purposes of distributed scaffolds.

- We can compare just-in-time and just-in-case scaffolds.

- We can describe the use of questions to check for understanding and to identify needed scaffolding.

- We can distinguish between types of prompts, cues, and direct explanations and modeling useful in distributed scaffolds.

How do you describe distributed scaffolds? Use the following question stems to jump-start your thinking.

- Who gets the distributed scaffolds?

- What signals do you look for and listen for to know when a distributed scaffold is needed?

- How do you monitor the effectiveness of distributed scaffolds?

At the risk of overusing the construction metaphor, let's quickly connect to what happens on a construction site using scaffolds. Of course, the scaffolds are erected in advance of workers engaging in their work. And different workers build the scaffolds compared with those who use the scaffolds to complete other tasks. In teaching, the same individual generally uses the *front-end*, *distributed*, and *back-end scaffolds,* so the construction metaphor only goes so far. Having said that, the workers who are completing tasks such as welding, painting, and so on do not only rely on the scaffolds put in place in advance of their presence on the site. They make regular adjustments to the scaffolding to accomplish their tasks.

In education, we call these the distributed scaffolds, or those that are being implemented, monitored, and adjusted during the learning process. These compare with *front-end scaffolds* that are enacted in advance of the learning. And they differ from those that are used *after* the learning tasks have been completed; these are the *back-end scaffolds* that will be the focus of Module 9.

Distributed scaffolding describes ongoing support through various tools, activities, technologies, and environments that increase student learning and performance (Puntambekar & Kolodner, 2005). Distributed scaffolding allows for different types and numbers of supports to be provided based on individual and group needs. In some cases, teachers need to provide just-in-time scaffolds based on students' errors and misunderstandings. In other cases, teachers can provide just-in-case scaffolds that they plan in advance of the learning tasks. When planning distributed scaffolds in advance, teachers note the common misconceptions students have in learning the specific content as well as their experiences with teaching this content previously and their experiences with the needs of this particular group of students. There are several different definitions of *just in time* and *just in case,* as the term is used in supply chains, inventory, and stock management to name a few. In terms of educational scaffolding, Dixon (2018) notes that

 Just-in-case scaffolds are provided to students before they attempt a challenging task

 Just-in-time scaffolds are provided when a student's struggle becomes unproductive, or they otherwise demonstrate they need help because they are unable to move forward

As we discussed in the previous module, front-end scaffolds that are *just in case* in nature can potentially reduce the rigor of the learning if used indiscriminately, and therefore should be used judiciously.

One example of a distributed scaffold that we integrated into this book is the inclusion of margin quotes. These are designed to highlight key ideas, and their formatting ensures that they stand out and help you to organize the content within the module. In doing so, these margin quotes help you to summarize and synthesize the information being presented. The effect size of outlining and summarizing is 0.71, above average in terms of the potential to increase learning. In this case, we've provided quotes that help you outline and summarize. However, actually creating the outline of the information or summarizing it in your own words would likely increase your retention of the information. Therefore, some of the interactive features in the modules provide you with opportunities to further consolidate information on your own.

QUESTIONS, PROMPTS, AND CUES

Distributed scaffolding relies, in part, on teacher actions that guide and support student thinking. As educators, we listen to and observe our students and then provide the nudges they need to get unstuck. These nudges can be classified as questions, prompts, and cues. And they typically occur in that order. Saying or doing the just-right thing so that the student does the cognitive work is a critical aspect of scaffolding. We will explore each of these types of distributed scaffolds in greater depth, but for now, let's work on some definitions. What do you think of when you read these terms in the context of scaffolding?

Questions

Prompts

Cues

Note that Figure 8.1 provides a flow chart for scaffolding with questions, prompts, and cues. This is a generalization of how distributed scaffolding works. Typically, we start with a question to check for understanding, and then we may ask additional questions to help students think. If that does not work, we consider prompts, which are statements that should spur thinking. If the questions and prompts don't work, we use cues, which are hints that focus or shift students' attention. And finally, if that does not work, we use direct explanations and modeling to support students. We'll explore the range of prompts and cues later in this module. For now, we will focus on the use of questions.

QUESTIONS

Posing questions is an essential move during distributed scaffolding. Questions help the teacher determine the extent to which previous instruction has "stuck." In other words, as teachers, we are continuously looking for evidence of uptake in learning.

The intention of the question is an important one, as the existence of a punctuation mark alone does not qualify the question as one useful in checking for understanding as part of distributed scaffolding. In some cases, questions are used to lead a learner, and those are more accurately described as prompts. A question posed to check for understanding yields a response that alerts the teacher about what a student knows and does not know at that moment in time. They are necessarily robust questions that are designed to work within a purposeful framework that moves beyond the Initiation-Response-Evaluation (IRE) cycle described by Cazden (2001) in which the teacher asks a question, receives a response, and then evaluates (correct or incorrect) before moving on. Students often describe IRE as "guess what's in the teacher's brain," and these questions are much less useful in determining the need for distributed scaffolds.

We have organized checking for understanding questions into six major categories, including those that elicit information, foster elaboration or clarification, require students to link divergent information, involve problem-solving heuristics, and trigger inventive responses (see Figure 8.2).

8.1 DISTRIBUTED SCAFFOLDING DECISION-MAKING TREE

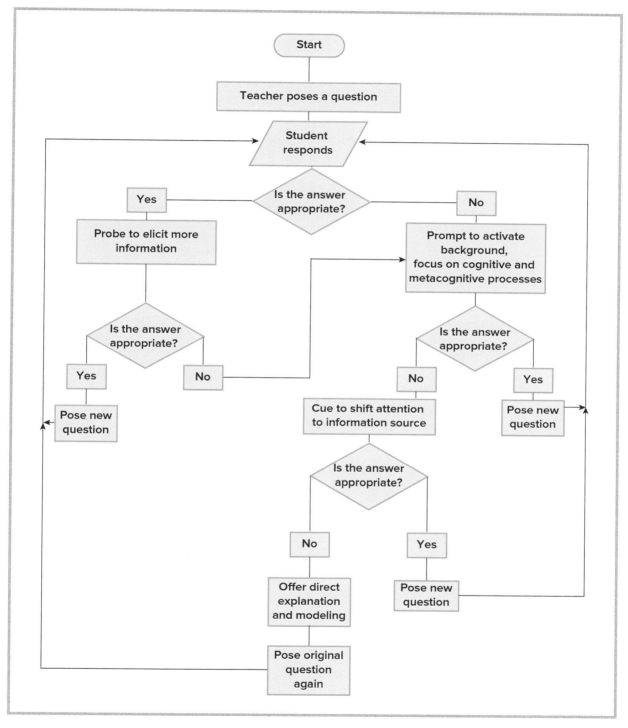

Source: Adapted from Frey and Fisher (2010).

8.2 TYPES OF QUESTIONS

Type of Question	Description
Elicitation questions	Elicitation questions invite the learner to offer information using concepts or skills that have been previously taught. This type of question is often phrased using familiar questions words: *who, what, when, where, why,* and *how.* They are used to unearth misconceptions and check for factual knowledge.
Elaboration questions	Elaboration questions often follow an initial elicitation as the teacher further probes student understanding. These questions are intended to increase the length of the response and allow students to do some thinking while talking. Often, explaining thinking helps both the speaker and the listener to figure out what went wrong.
Clarification questions	As with elaboration questions, these are frequently paired with initial elicitation questions and are intended to further expose the student's knowledge of the content. These questions allow the teacher to gain further details about students' understanding.
Divergent questions	Divergent questions require the learner to consolidate concepts about two topics to create a new relationship. The teacher's intent in this case is to discover how the student uses existing knowledge to formulate a new understanding.
Heuristic questions	Sometimes the focus of the question is on students' ability to formulate an informal problem-solving technique. Heuristics, also described as a rule of thumb, are techniques learners use as they address and solve a problem.
Inventive questions	These questions invite students to use what they have learned to speculate or create. They stimulate imaginative thought and can unearth misconceptions.

❋ Use What You Know

Given the descriptions of various question types in Figure 8.2, identify the type of question in each of the following situations. Our answers are at the end of the module. Note that these questions would be used to identify distributed scaffolds that would keep students' learning moving forward.

Situation	Type of Question
1. Can you tell me more about that?	
2. Teacher points to a sentence strip and asks, "What is the verb in this sentence?"	
3. Where might you see the aurora borealis?	
4. Why does water look blue in a lake, but clear in a glass?	

Situation	Type of Question
5. Can you show or explain where you found the information and why it supports the answer?	
6. If you could, what advice would you have given to George Washington during the winter at Valley Forge?	
7. Do butterflies and moths have anything in common?	
8. How could you figure out the meaning of this word: word parts or context clues?	
9. Why did you choose that answer?	
10. Why might the Sierra Nevada mountain range be called "the backbone of the state"?	
11. How do you know when you have run out of ways to answer this question?	
12. Who would you recommend this book to?	

As students respond to these questions, teachers listen and identify errors, misunderstandings, and misconceptions. Once identified, distributed scaffolding is put into play. Again, in this module, we are focused on scaffolds that occur *during* the learning process rather than scaffolds that were enacted in advance of the learning experience or scaffolds that are applied after the learning experience has been completed.

PROMPTS TO GUIDE THINKING

During distributed scaffolding, the teacher makes an initial inquiry to check for understanding and may ask further questions to cause the student to extend, elaborate, or clarify. When students are not able to respond correctly, or their responses demonstrate partial understanding, additional scaffolds are necessary. This comes in the form of prompts, which are statements or questions that assist the student in focusing on the cognitive or metacognitive processes needed to complete the task. Unlike questions to check for understanding, prompts are intended to get the student to do the thinking needed to achieve a new level of understanding. Prompts can be organized into four broad categories:

1. Background knowledge
2. Process or procedural knowledge
3. Models, templates, or frames
4. Reflective knowledge

Figure 8.3 contains a description of each of these types of prompts and examples.

8.3 TYPES OF PROMPTS

Type of Prompt	Definition/ When to Use	Examples
Background knowledge	Used when there is content that the student already knows, has been taught, or has experienced but has temporarily forgotten or is using incorrectly.	• As part of a science passage about the water cycle, the teacher asks, "What do you remember about states of matter?" • When reading about a trip to the zoo, the teacher asks, "Remember when we had a field trip to the zoo last month? Do you recall how we felt when it started to rain?"
Process or procedure	Used when established or generally agreed-on rules or guidelines are not being followed and a reminder will help resolve the error or misconception.	• The student is saying a word incorrectly, and the teacher says, "When two vowels go walking . . ." • When the student has difficulty starting to develop a writing outline, the teacher says, "I'm thinking about the mnemonic we've used for organizing an explanatory article."
Reflective	Used to encourage students to be metacognitive and to think about their thinking, which can then be used to determine the next steps or the solution to a problem.	• The student has just read something incorrectly, and the teacher asks, "Does that make sense? Look at all of the letters. Really think about it." • When the student fails to include evidence in her writing, the teacher asks, "What are we learning today? What was our purpose?"
Heuristic	Used to help learners develop their own way to solve problems. These are informal problem-solving procedures. They do not have to be the same as others' heuristics, but they do need to work.	• When the student has difficulty explaining the relationships between characters in a text, the teacher says, "Maybe drawing a visual representation of the main character's connections to others will help you." • When a student gets stuck and cannot think of what to write next, the teacher says, "Writers have a lot of different ways of getting unstuck. Some just write whatever comes to mind, others create a visual, others talk it out with a reader, and others take a break and walk around for a few minutes. Will any of those help you?"

Source: Adapted from Fisher and Frey (2013).

Here is an example to illustrate the use of prompts. During a reading of the novel *Esperanza Rising* (Ryan, 2002), a fifth-grade teacher asked about the use of symbolism. The students in their literature circle had read the latest chapter but were having difficulty relating the events to a previously taught symbol in the story.

"I'm going to remind you about how important the blanket her *abuelita* is making is," he remarked. "That zigzag pattern is important."

One student responded, "Yeah, yeah, it's like ups and downs and ups and downs."

The teacher encouraged him to make the connection to a new event in the chapter. "Right! Now use that! How does that zigzag relate to what just happened to Esperanza?"

The student then replied, "It's a bad time because she got called 'Cinderella' for doing such a bad job sweeping up the onion skins off the floor. She was used to being treated like a princess or something, and now things are just going straight downhill for her." As he said this, he tilted his arm in a downward slant. The strategic use of a background knowledge prompt helped this learner reach a deeper understanding of the text.

Similarly, when the teacher questioned students about their physics project, a misconception about speed versus velocity was uncovered. In prompting them, the teacher said, "Remember the animation we watched about driving to school? Velocity and speed have some things in common, but . . ." The students immediately responded with a quote from the animation—"velocity is speed with direction"—and their misconception was resolved.

 ## Use What You Know

Using the descriptions of various types of prompts in Figure 8.3, identify the specific type for each of the following situations. Our answers are at the end of the module. For the blank example, identify a situation in which that type of prompting would be appropriate.

Situation	Type of Prompt
1. A group of students was stuck on a math problem and their teacher prompted them with a reminder to apply **PEMDAS** (the order of operations) rather than tell them where they had made their mistake.	
2. A student explained that they didn't understand the passage and couldn't write a summary. The teacher asked, "What can you do to help yourself?"	
3.	Background knowledge

CUING STUDENTS' ATTENTION

Another instructional move that scaffolds understanding involves shifts of learner attention. These differ from prompts in that they are more directly related to what the student is noticing, or not noticing, rather than focused on the cognitive or metacognitive processes the student needs to use. Using cues, the teacher diverts the learner's attention to a source of information that will help the student solve a problem or to highlight an error or misunderstanding.

There are a number of cues that teachers use, including visual, verbal, gestural/ physical, and environmental. Regardless of the mode, cues provide the learner with additional information about what to notice. See Figure 8.4 for a list of cues.

8.4 TYPES OF CUES

Type of Cue	Definition	Example
Visual	A range of graphic hints that guide students through thinking or understanding.	• Highlighting places on a text where students have made errors • Creating a graphic organizer to arrange content visually • Asking students to take a second look at a graphic or visual from a textbook
Verbal	Variations in speech are used to draw attention to something specific or verbal attention-getters that focus students' thinking.	• "This is important . . ." • "This is the tricky part. Be careful and be sure to . . ." • Repeating a student's statement using a questioning intonation • Changing volume or speed of speech for emphasis
Gestural/ Physical	The teacher's body movements or motions are used to draw attention to something that has been missed.	• Pointing to the word wall when a student is searching for the right word or the spelling of a word • Making a hand motion that has been taught in advance such as the one used to indicate the importance of summarizing or predicting while reading • Placing thumbs around a key idea in a text that the student was missing
Environmental	Using the surroundings, and things in the surroundings, to influence students' understanding.	• Keeping environmental print current so that students can use it as a reference • Using magnetic letters or other manipulatives to guide students' thinking • Moving an object or person so that the orientation changes and guides thinking

Source: Adapted from Fisher and Frey (2013).

A few additional examples will illustrate the use of cues. The following questions are examples of *visual cues* that shift learners' attention to something that may help them respond. Essentially, these are hints that support learners rather than telling them the information that they are missing.

Visual Cues

→ Who's in the background of this picture? Why?

→ The information in the chart might help you. Take a look again.

→ Take a minute to review the pictures you've seen so far before you make a prediction about how you think the story will end.

→ See how they made this look like a button? They want you to click that for the answer.

→ Based on the way the artist drew this character, are you sure he's happy about this?

→ When you get to a heading, what does that remind you to do?

Gestural cues are also commonly used.

Gestural Cues

→ The teacher points to information on a language chart without saying anything. The student rereads the chart and is able to add to the discussion he was having with his group.

→ A teacher uses her hands in a chopping motion when reminding a student to chunk words as she sounds them out.

→ A teacher motions larger or bigger by starting with her hands close together and moving them apart. As she does so, the student starts talking again, expanding on his ideas for responding to the writing prompt.

✳ Use What You Know

Given the descriptions of various types of cues in Figure 8.4, identify the specific type for each of the following situations on the next page. Our answers are at the end of the module. For the blank examples, identify a situation in which that type of cuing would be appropriate.

Situation	Type of Cue
1. Saying, "Take a look at the figure on page 112. Does that help?"	
2. Giving a touch to the shoulder to divert the student's gaze to the left	
3. Reminding a student to use a sound word wall to identify how to spell a word	
4. Pointing to a graph, saying, "Population *per* thousand" emphasizing with your voice the word *per*	
5. Correcting a student's grip on the baseball bat by moving the student's hands	
6.	Verbal
7.	Environmental

PROVIDING DIRECT EXPLANATIONS AND MODELING

Sometimes, prompts and cues do not resolve the errors or misconceptions that students have. In those cases, students cannot be left hanging. Teachers must ensure that students have a successful learning experience, even if that means providing a direct explanation and giving the student the answer. Importantly, direct explanations should come after prompts and cues to increase the likelihood that students can connect this new information to a thinking process in which they were engaged. Following the direct explanation, the teacher should monitor students' understanding by asking them to repeat the information back in their own words or asking the original question they used to check for understanding. These direct explanations are consistent with those Thompson (2009) offered: "giving explanations, examples, or the answer; explaining the answer; referring to a previous discussion; posing a leading question for the student; and planning what the student should do next" (p. 427).

For example, a group of five third-grade students was reading *Voices in the Park* (Browne, 1998). After checking for understanding and realizing that Nichole was relying on the illustrations to make her predictions rather than the words in the text, and after prompting and cuing her to use the author's words, the teacher moved to direct explanation: "Illustrations can help us make predictions, but they don't always give us a complete picture. Readers also have to use the *words* they read to make predictions. The words *scruffy mongrel* and *horrible thing* give me a different picture in my mind than what I see in the picture. Use those words to make your prediction."

One of the ways that teachers can provide direct explanations is through modeling. As part of modeling, "the teacher explicitly states which strategy is being taught and when it will be used. Then the teacher applies a think-aloud model that includes the reasoning involved in using the strategy, thereby revealing his or her [thinking] processes" (Alfassi, 2004, p. 172). For example, when students were having difficulty writing introductions and prompts and cues did not help, the teacher took out a piece of paper and wrote a sample introduction, thinking aloud as she did so. Her think-aloud included conscious decisions about which introduction techniques to use and how to vary sentence starters and sentence length. As part of her modeling, the teacher said,

> Given that my topic is comparing two fairy tales, I don't think that using humor as an introduction type is a good idea because my reader might not take me seriously. I'm also thinking that a startling statistic won't work as I don't know one about fairy tales. I do think asking a question might work in this case, because it will get my reader interested in the topic. And I'm thinking that a quote might work, but then I'm not really sure where I would get a quote, since there are two fairy tales. Maybe I'll save that idea for later in my paper. Okay, so I made a decision. I'm going to start with a question. I'll start my introduction by saying, "Have you ever wondered why some of the same characters act differently in different stories?" Then I can compare the two versions of "Cinderella" that I read.

Note that the teacher modeling included two important components. The first is "I" statements and the second focuses on the ways in which the teacher accomplished this task. The "I" statements invite students to listen emphatically as their teacher opens up their brains to show how they accomplished the task. But providing examples is not sufficient. Students have already been prompted and cued. They need to know how the teacher did this because thinking is invisible. The teacher's thinking is contextualized with examples of how the teacher accomplished the task.

And note, direct explanations and modeling are brief. They are used to ensure that students experience success—productive success. When we resort to modeling, it's often an indicator that additional instruction is needed. But in the moment, we want to ensure that students are successful so that they do not experience unproductive failure and start to think of themselves as incapable of learning.

These are important points about scaffolding. When learning with the teacher, students need to feel a sense of accomplishment, even if the teacher has to directly explain something. If not, the student is likely to think, "It can't be my teacher, it must be me. I must be stupid." When that happens, students develop learned helplessness and become dependent on adults for information. That's the exact opposite of what we hope for when we use distributed scaffolds.

COACH A PEER

This feature is an opportunity for you to try out new learning. We'll give you a short scenario about a teacher whose instruction might benefit from your knowledge about distributed scaffolds.

Emily Jensen, a sixth-grade social studies teacher, is teaching her students about ancient Egypt. Her students were learning about the hieroglyphic system of writing developed by the ancient Egyptians. She instructed her students about specific vocabulary and had them independently read a passage from the textbook on hieroglyphics. Ms. Jensen then introduced a partner discussion to summarize the reading with one another.

"I want to hear these words in your conversation: *hieroglyphics*, *writing system*, and *civilization*," she reminded them. Near the end of the lesson, she asked students to write an exit slip summarizing their learning. She posted on the board:

> Please write a paragraph summary about what you learned today: The reason writing is so important to civilizations is _____. For example, the ancient Egyptians _____. This reminds me of _____.

However, when she reviewed the exit slips after school, she saw that a significant portion of her students did not complete the task accurately. She grouped the errors into two major categories:

- Those who were not able to explain why writing was essential to this civilization.

- Those who could not link this to previously taught civilizations, such as cave paintings among the Neanderthals, or cuneiforms in ancient Persia.

Ms. Jensen meets with you about the results, asking you for advice about what she might do more effectively to check for understanding. Use what you know about robust questions, prompts, and cues to make suggestions about what the teacher could do during instruction using distributed scaffolds.

CONCLUSION

Distributed scaffolds are harder to plan for than front-end scaffolds because they are used in response to a learner's needs—they are just-in-time. But they are not impossible to plan. With experience, teachers can anticipate the types of errors and misconceptions that students may have while learning specific content. As we plan lessons, then, we think about this and how we might respond. The goal is not to simply tell students whatever it is that they are missing, but rather to provide supports—scaffolds—while students are engaged in learning tasks.

The distributed scaffolds that were highlighted in this module include questions, prompts, cues, and direct explanations. Each of these has a role to play as students engage in learning tasks. Teachers are always on the lookout for needs to scaffold as students are learning, moving us closer and closer to success. It's an ongoing process of providing these supports, in combination with the front-end and back-end scaffolds.

SELF-ASSESSMENT

Before moving forward, consider the success criteria for this module. You will notice these statements have been revised from "We can" statements to "Can I?" questions. Using the traffic light scale, with red being not confident, yellow being somewhat confident, and green indicating very confident, how confident are you in your ability to utilize knowledge of distributed scaffolds? You'll also want to take note of evidence you have for your self-assessment.

SUCCESS CRITERIA	SELF-ASSESSMENT	EVIDENCE
Can I define the meaning and purposes of distributed scaffolds?		
Can I compare just-in-time and just-in-case scaffolds?		
Can I describe the use of questions to check for understanding and to identify needed scaffolding?		
Can I distinguish between types of prompts, cues, and direct explanations and modeling useful in distributed scaffolds?		

Answers to questions for **Use What You Know—Questions**:

1. Elaboration
2. Elicitation
3. Elicitation
4. Divergent
5. Clarification
6. Inventive
7. Divergent
8. Heuristic
9. Clarification
10. Divergent
11. Heuristic
12. Inventive

Answers to questions for **Use What You Know—Prompts**:

1. Process or procedure
2. Reflective

Answers to questions for **Use What You Know—Cues**:

1. Said verbally, but is a visual cue
2. Physical
3. Environmental
4. Verbal
5. Physical

Access resources, tools, and guides
for this module at the companion website:
resources.corwin.com/howscaffoldingworks

9

BACK-END SCAFFOLDS

LEARNING INTENTION

We are learning about scaffolds that are used after learning events have occurred so that learning is extended, or errors are corrected.

SUCCESS CRITERIA

We will know we are successful when

- We can determine the differences between front-end, distributed, and back-end scaffolds.

- We can use graphic organizers as a back-end scaffold to help students move from surface to deeper learning.

- We can explore the ways in which study skills can be used as a back-end scaffold to help students move from surface to deeper learning.

- We can explain the conditions necessary for feedback to work.

- We can explain the three components of feedback that increase its usefulness as a back-end scaffold.

How do you describe back-end scaffolds? Use the following question stems to jump-start your thinking.

- What actions can you take when learning does not occur as intended?

(Continued)

(Continued)

- When might scaffolds be most effective after tasks have been completed?

- What role might feedback play in serving as a scaffold?

Thus far, we have used the construction scaffold analogy to explain and explore educational scaffolds. Generally, in construction, the scaffolds are attached to a more permanent structure, such as a building. Scaffolds are erected, used, and then dismantled because the structure underneath is what is important. For most of us, that's the type of scaffold we think about when we hear the word. But there is another type of scaffold: scaffolding stairs. These are self-contained units—stairs—that can be moved from place to place. In other words, this type of scaffold moves as needed.

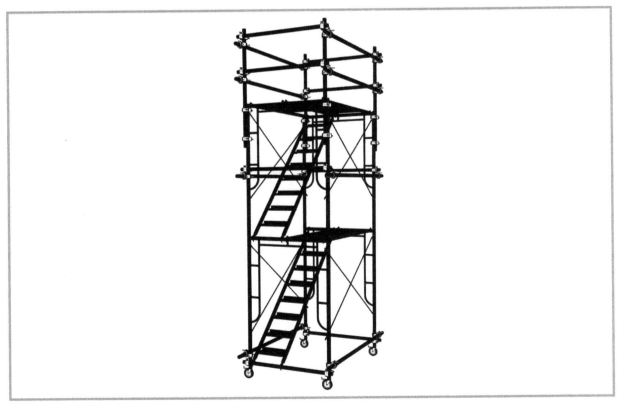

Source: Graphic courtesy of iStock.com/Ninja Artist

Think about the airport. Often, there is a jet bridge that allows passengers to disembark from the plane. But sometimes, there is no jet bridge, and a set of stairs are rolled up to the side of the plane to allow people to exit safely. This happens after the fact; the flying has already occurred. Sometimes, the ground crew knows that a specific gate will require boarding stairs, and other times something happens, and these temporary scaffolding stairs are used.

We would consider these back-end scaffolds or supports that are enacted after the learning experience has occurred. In some cases, back-end scaffolds are used to correct misconceptions and errors that were not addressed during the learning process. As an example, providing feedback to students can be a back-end scaffold used to keep students learning. In other cases, back-end scaffolds are used to solidify students' understanding following the learning experience. For example, inviting students to graphically organize information can serve as a back-end scaffold that extends learning as students see the relationships and connections between ideas and information.

Regardless of the time in which scaffolds are used, front-end, distributed, or back-end, EL Education (n.d.) suggests that they need to meet specific criteria. Scaffolds should be

- Sensitive to students' strengths and challenges
- Standards-based
- In alignment with learning targets
- Applied to the process of meeting the learning target
- Temporary
- Used to provide a student with necessary supports to accomplish a task that is not otherwise possible
- Appropriate to the task
- Respectful for all learners

Use What You Know

Consider the following potential scaffolds. Do they meet the criteria listed above? Note that these are not necessarily all back-end scaffolds, but rather include knowledge gained from previous modules.

Potential Scaffold	Does It Meet EL Education Criteria?
1. Placing students in homogeneous work groups to complete a collaborative task.	
2. Providing "hint cards" that students can use to get unstuck so that they get the gist of the information.	
3. Identifying vocabulary from a video clip that students struggled with and reviewing those terms following the experience.	
4. Providing a teacher think-aloud so that students can revise their work based on the examples provided.	
5. Providing students who struggled in the previous unit with modified versions of the text to read.	

GRAPHIC ORGANIZERS AS BACK-END SCAFFOLDS

Graphic organizers are visual and spatial displays that assist students in classifying abstract concepts in ways that highlight their relationship to one another. They are used to help learners build schemas, which are cognitive frameworks for understanding and interpreting information. Naive learners can incorrectly view knowledge as silos of unrelated facts, as when a science student is not able to see the relationship between the lesson on planetary movement and the previous one on planetary composition. Importantly, their intended use is to foster links between prior knowledge and new information (Ausubel, 1968).

However, graphic organizers in practice are widely misused. Two common mistakes undermine their effectiveness: function and timing (Fisher & Frey, 2018). The first is when the graphic organizer is narrowly viewed as being the end product. Filling out the graphic organizer becomes the end goal. Students turn it in, the lesson continues, and the opportunity to build schemas is forgotten. Graphic organizers should be understood as an intermediate tool to something else, most often discussion and writing (Fisher & Frey, 2018).

Graphic organizers should be understood as an intermediate tool to something else, most often discussion and writing.

The second error is in timing, and here's where back-end scaffolding becomes relevant. In some cases, the use of the graphic organizer is premature. The teacher introduces a lesson and then displays a completed graphic organizer for students to copy. Rather than considering conceptual relationships, they are focused instead on filling in all the little boxes so that it matches the teacher's sample. And guess who has done all the thinking? It's the teacher, who considered the relationships between ideas, classified them into categories, and selected the graphic organizer that would best represent these ideas spatially and visually.

We'd like to separate graphic organizers from an adjunct display that offers a pictorial representation of new information to be taught. These are a form of front-end scaffolding in that they are intended to be used at the outset as a part of initial instruction. Providing a representational picture of the solar system makes a lot of sense when introducing planetary movement. Using an accompanying chart so that students can compare and contrast the relative sizes and properties of the planets makes sense when providing instruction about planetary composition.

But the usefulness of a graphic organizer emerges when students must construct linkages about the relationships between the concepts being taught. For instance, a student-constructed graphic organizer comparing Mercury and Venus in terms of rotation and revolution, as well as their temperature and geological features, is a different task. It requires that the student link two major ideas—planetary movement and composition—and further expand it to compare to another planet. There is significant thinking—not just copying—that the student must accomplish in order to sort out information, categorize and classify knowledge, and apply it as a conceptual framework to better understand the other planets.

The use of a graphic organizer after an initial lesson or reading has been completed allows learners to sort out what they know and bring to light what they don't know or are confused about. One meta-analysis on the use of graphic organizers after instruction was striking. When used *after* lessons, the effect size was 1.84 (Englert & Mariage, 1991). When used generically in the lesson, the effect size is only 0.61. These don't have to be tremendously complex, either. Figure 9.1 is a middle school student's attempt to figure out the character traits and actions of Jackie, the protagonist in *Brown Girl Dreaming* (Woodson, 2016). It's important to note that this is a work in progress. As the student reads, and lessons evolve, they return to the graphic organizer to continue to build their understanding of the main character.

9.1 **CHARACTER ANALYSIS OF JACKIE**

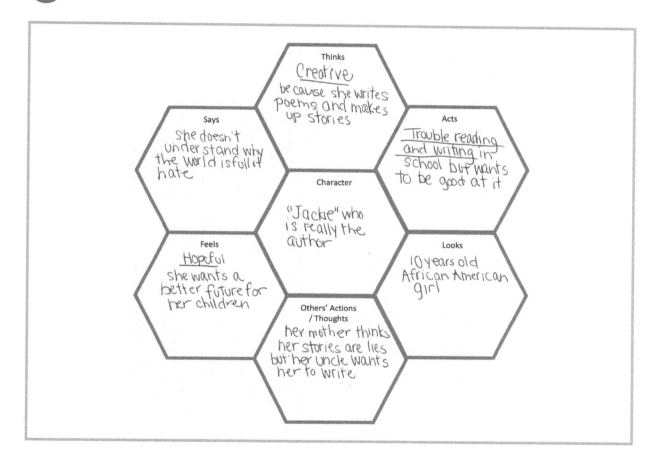

Graphic organizers can also be an effective tool for study, as we will discuss further in the next section of the module. This is especially true for older students who are building graphic organizers incrementally, as they become a good repository for their deepening understanding of a concept. One of the important skills they must learn over time is how to align the function of a particular graphic organizer with their purpose.

✳ Use What You Know

There are a number of different types of graphic organizers and their functions vary in terms of the ways that they organize conceptual thinking. Consider these four types of graphic organizers, giving consideration as to how you might use them as a bridge to discussion or writing. Use the blank column to capture ideas useful in your grade level or subject.

Function	Types	Discussion Application	Writing Application
Outline	• Timeline • Semantic maps • Flow chart • Sequence chart • Spider map • Cycle map		
Compare-contrast	• Matrix • Venn • T-chart		
Hierarchical	• Tree diagram • Thematic map • Fishbone map		
Relational	• Bubble map • Semantic feature analysis • Problem-solution		

STUDY SKILLS

Study skills are a constellation of competencies that allow students to acquire, record, organize, synthesize, remember, and use information (Hoover & Patton, 1995). Study skills are important in learning content, and they are transferable, allowing students to apply what they have learned in new situations. We think of study skills as a back-end scaffold because students who know how to study do so after the initial learning has occurred. This is an important point. We don't want students to use study skills while they are learning new content. The focus during initial learning should be on acquiring concepts and skills. Rather, study skills should be used to solidify the learning on the back end to ensure that students move into deeper learning and transfer of learning.

Hattie (2009) suggested that study skills could be organized into three categories: *cognitive*, *metacognitive*, and *affective*.

➡ **Cognitive study skills** usually involve a task, such as reviewing notes, creating digital or physical flashcards, and summarizing.

➡ **Metacognitive study skills** describe self-management, such as planning, monitoring, and reflecting on studying. Metacognitive study skills also require that students learn when to use various cognitive strategies.

➡ **Affective study skills** involve motivation, agency, and self-concept.

An example of cognitive study skills is mnemonics, which is an aid often using initial letters to help activate memory. While learning the cardinal points of the compass, students in a first-grade class were introduced to the mnemonic "Never Eat Shredded Wheat" to associate the directions in the correct order clockwise starting at the top.

But as Mr. Saunders said to his class, "I really like shredded wheat, so I don't like to try to remember the directions with this saying. How about each table group come up with a different mnemonic that they can use to remember this information?"

One of the groups came up with "No Evidence Sorry Writers" and another group suggested, "Never Eat Shaved Walrus."

Another example of *cognitive* study skills is the use of flashcards. This sounds very old school, but flashcards (and their digital equivalents such as Anki, Quizlet, or Cram) can help students remember information. Of course, they need to do more than remember information, but remembering is important. For example, students used *IDoRecall*, which allows users to create flashcards with text, pictures, and video. During their investigation of biomes, students were focused on diverse life forms from different environments. The students created a series of flashcards so that they could remember the various biomes, the environmental conditions of those biomes, and the types of animals that lived in the environment. In creating the flashcards, students were studying the biomes. And in practicing with their flashcards, they were continuing to think about the content they were expected to learn.

An example of *metacognitive* study skills is self-evaluation. Understanding one's current level of performance and being able to identify learning needs is another study skill that students need to develop. For students to successfully self-evaluate, teachers have to be very clear about what success looks like for a given task. Importantly, teachers can start small and provide students feedback with their early attempts to self-evaluate. During a science lesson on the relative positions of objects, students were provided with several visuals, and they had to decide which words were appropriate for describing the relative position of the item in question. Students were expected to use specific terminology to describe the position of a targeted item, and their teacher informed them of the success criteria:

> We know that we will be successful when we use these terms [pointing to a list of terms on the wall, such as distal, medial, and posterior] and correctly describe the position of specific objects.

We don't want students to use study skills while they are learning new content.

The teacher took pictures of each example and then asked students to check themselves by looking at the picture he displayed on his smart board. Once they had checked themselves, the teacher asked students to trade papers with a partner and compare answers. He rotated through the images again so that the students could talk about their answers. He then invited a member from each partnership to collect several objects from the collection he had so that they could place them on their desks and discuss the relative position of each. They took photos using a tablet and wrote on the image using the targeted vocabulary. Learning to check builds an eventual skill of self-evaluation.

Cognitive and metacognitive study skills are important, but engagement, motivation, and self-concept are also important. To our thinking, motivation requires success. When we experience success, we are more motivated to keep at something. When we think about study skills, we are reminded that all too often, students are not successful. They fail the test they studied for, or they do not produce a report of information that has sufficient evidence. It's not very motivating for them to try again. That's why it's important to consider *affective* study skills.

Wise teachers are careful to ensure that students experience success when they introduce study skills. For example, students were preparing for an exam that included a variety of question types. Each night, the teacher provided students with a specific type of question (e.g., short answer, multiple choice) and content that could be assessed using that question type. She provided students with examples and asked them to study. She gave them a practice assessment the next day and allowed them to score their responses and identify errors. They were encouraged to talk with peers about their thinking. The students experienced significant success and were motivated to keep trying. Their scores on the "real" test were impressive, but even more so was their motivation to study and their ability to learn information and then apply that information in the projects they completed the following week.

As this teacher noted, "It's really important to me that students experience early success because they start to think of themselves as scholars. Then I can increase my expectations and they always rise to them."

✳ Use What You Know

Place the following items in the appropriate category of study skills: cognitive, meta-cognitive, or affective. Note that these are written as "I can" statements, as we encourage students to develop these skills and then select when to use them. In this way, study skills become a back-end scaffold that students deploy on their own.

➡ I can use my comprehension strategies when I am not sure that I understood what I read.

➡ I can make sure that I am in a good spot to learn.

➡ I can make a plan for my project.

➡ I can make flashcards.

➡ I can review vocabulary words to make sure I know what they mean.

➡ I can memorize important information.

➡ I can summarize what I read.

➡ I can correct my mistakes.

➡ I can keep track of my own learning.

➡ I can make sure that I have enough time for my assignment.

➡ I can make changes to my work.

➡ I can self-assess my work.

➡ I can reread.

➡ I can take notes.

➡ I can be excited to learn.

➡ I can keep track of my understanding.

➡ I can get through a challenge.

➡ I can set goals.

➡ I can be ready to solve problems.

➡ I can use a graphic organizer.

➡ I can use self-questioning.

Cognitive Study Skills	Metacognitive Study Skills	Affective Study Skills

FEEDBACK

Much has been written about feedback (e.g., Hattie & Clark, 2019) and the complexities of this teaching move. As Covey (1995) noted, "It takes humility to seek feedback. It takes wisdom to understand it, analyze it and appropriately act on it." The reality is that much feedback is given, but not all that feedback is received. When it's not received, it does little to promote learning. Perhaps the reason is that feedback is given prematurely in the instructional cycle. Note that we place feedback in the back-end scaffold section and not in the distributed scaffold section. Of course, teachers can give feedback while students are learning, especially in the form of reinforcement and cues. But feedback can also be used to address errors and misconceptions after the learning tasks have been completed.

We have argued that planning feedback requires that teachers attend to:

➡ *Care*: The establishment and maintenance of a learning atmosphere of trust and respect. When care is absent, students are guarded and may not expose their misunderstandings or be willing to accept feedback as a growth-producing event.

➡ *Credibility*: The belief that the other person is worthy of listening to and learning from. Essentially, students ask themselves, "Can I learn from this person?" If the answer is yes, then feedback is much more likely to have an impact.

➡ *Clarity*: The understanding that there are things worth learning, what that learning is, and what it means to successfully learn. When these conditions are present, learners are much more likely to accept the feedback because they see it as valuable for the goals they have agreed to and desire to accomplish.

➡ *Communication*: The way in which the message is sent and whether or not learners can understand, and act on, the information shared.

In other words, Almarode et al. (2023, p. 96) state that

➡ Care and credibility set the foundation for **who** is giving, receiving, and integrating the feedback

➡ Clarity sets the foundation for **what** feedback is given, received, and integrated

➡ Communication sets the foundation for **how** the feedback is given

With these in mind, teachers are ready to use feedback as a back-end scaffold. Remember, feedback provides information about how someone is doing as they progress toward a desired goal. You'll recall that mental models of expertise and goals are part of the scaffolding and practice framework that guides this book. As Vrabie (2021) noted, feedback comes in at least three forms:

1. **Appreciation:** *Recognizing* and *rewarding* someone for great work. Appreciation *connects* and *motivates people,* and it's vital since *intrinsic motivation* is one of the critical factors for *high performance.*

2. **Coaching:** *Helping* someone expand their knowledge, skills, and capabilities. Coaching is also an opportunity to *address feelings,* which helps balance and strengthen *relationships.*

3. **Evaluation:** *Assessing* someone against a set of standards, aligning expectations and informing decision making.

Notice that each of these can be useful in back-end scaffolding. When we appreciate what students have accomplished rather than only focusing on learning needs, we motivate them to try again even when they face obstacles. When we coach, we provide specific examples and ideas that students can use to expand their skills and develop habits. And when we evaluate, we compare students' current performance with the expectation for learning. Notice that these are not linear. We may start with appreciation or end with it. We may base the coaching on the evaluation. We may vacillate between these three moves as we scaffold students' learning.

Ninth-grade teacher Michael Quezada is teaching an introductory unit on culture and identity in his Ethnic Studies course. His students are reading the article "Body Ritual Among the Nacirema" (Miner, 1956), which describes a culture in anthropological terms, explaining the group's fixation with oral cleanliness and attitudes about the body. After their initial reading and discussion of the essay, Mr. Quezada revealed that the culture in question is really "American" spelled backward, a detail none of the students had figured out. He then connected this satire to the tendency to discuss other cultures as having only one major identity, such as *machismo* in Spanish cultures or *face* in some Asian cultures. The teacher then asks his students to add their reactions and questions to the Padlet he has set up for his students to use.

As he watches the real-time collaborative organizer evolve, he makes note of specific entries as he provides feedback. He offers appreciation (e.g., "Mariel said that the reading caused her surprise because she never thought of an American culture this way. Thanks, Mariel. You voiced what a lot of others are saying."). In addition, some of his feedback is in the form of coaching (e.g., "Four of you wondered about other examples of cultures that are reduced to a single quality. Let's keep an eye out for those examples as we move through this unit. We can keep a list of those we encounter in our readings."). Mr. Quezada also provides an evaluation statement as feedback to the group. "I can see by your questions and comments that you are already beginning to cultivate a stance of cultural analysis. That's going to be an important lens that we'll return to again and again as we explore the experiences of different groups in America."

✳ Use What You Know

Building new habits takes time. When we started using feedback as a back-end scaffold, we planned some of the actions and conversations that we thought we might use to increase students' likelihood of learning from the feedback. Consider an upcoming series of lessons and how you might think about the three forms of feedback. Develop some sentence starters that align with each of these that you might use to ensure that this type of scaffolding works.

Forms of Feedback	
Appreciation	
Coaching	
Evaluation	

COACH A PEER

This feature is an opportunity for you to try out new learning. We'll give you a short scenario about a teacher whose instruction might benefit from your knowledge about back-end scaffolds.

Leticia Ramos is planning a series of lessons about the water cycle that will require students to take notes. Ms. Ramos requires that her students use Cornell notes, which require that pages be divided into three sections. The major column is on the left, a minor column on the right, and space at the bottom across the two columns. Notes are taken in the major column, key ideas or terms from the notes are included in the minor column, and summaries are written at the bottom of the page. To serve as a study skill, the minor column and summary are completed after the notes are taken, often days later to aid in the recall and organization of information.

One day, the students watched a short video that was included in the instructional materials the district had purchased. Ms. Ramos asked her students to take notes during the video to encourage active involvement. Because they had used Cornell notes before, the students immediately took out their science notebooks, added an entry in the table of contents, and turned to a blank page, ready to collect information.

What scaffolds might Ms. Ramos consider as students watch the video (distributed scaffolds)?

What scaffolds might Ms. Ramos consider after the video has been seen (back-end scaffolds)?

CONCLUSION

This module has focused on some of the actions that teachers can take after learning events have occurred. In some cases, back-end scaffolds are used to address misconceptions and errors. Of course, there are times in which errors are global, meaning that the majority of the class misunderstood something. In those cases, re-teaching is probably warranted. In other cases, feedback can be used to address incomplete learning. In addition, back-end scaffolds are useful in helping students consolidate their understanding. In these cases, the surface learning that students have completed can be extended into deeper learning through intentional back-end scaffolds. Effective teachers use the trifecta of scaffolding—front-end, distributed, and back-end—to ensure that students are learning. As students experience scaffolding, they begin to scaffold the learning of their peers, which is the focus of the next module.

SELF-ASSESSMENT

Before moving forward, consider the success criteria for this module. You will notice these statements have been revised from "We can" statements to "Can I?" questions. Using the traffic light scale, with red being not confident, yellow being somewhat confident, and green indicating very confident, how confident are you in your ability to utilize knowledge of back-end scaffolds? You'll also want to take note of evidence you have for your self-assessment.

SUCCESS CRITERIA	SELF-ASSESSMENT	EVIDENCE
Can I determine the differences between front-end, distributed, and back-end scaffolds?		
Can I use graphic organizers as a back-end scaffold to help students move from surface to deeper learning?		
Can I explore the ways in which study skills can be used as a back-end scaffold to help students move from surface to deeper learning?		
Can I explain the conditions necessary for feedback to work?		
Can I explain the three components of feedback that increase its usefulness as a back-end scaffold?		

Answers to questions for **Use What You Know—EL Education Criteria for Scaffolding:**

1. No, not respectful for all learners and may not allow all students to access grade-level standards.

2. Yes, they are available to all and are sensitive to student challenges.

3. Yes, it is temporary and aligned with the learning target. Vocabulary could have also been taught as a front-end scaffold, but in this case, there were terms that were not expected to be confusing.

4. Yes, used to provide necessary supports to accomplish the learning targets.

5. No, not standards aligned, and it may be possible to have students access a complex text in other ways, but this may be done as part of the support for a student with an identified disability.

Answers to questions for **Use What You Know—Study Skills:**

COGNITIVE STUDY SKILLS	METACOGNITIVE STUDY SKILLS	AFFECTIVE STUDY SKILLS
I can use a graphic organizer.	I can keep track of my own learning.	I can be excited to learn.
I can take notes.	I can make a plan for my project.	I can make sure that I have enough time for my assignment.
I can summarize what I read.	I can correct my mistakes.	I can get through a challenge.
I can make flashcards.	I can make changes to my work.	I can make sure that I am in a good spot to learn.
I can reread.	I can self-assess my work.	I can set goals.
I can memorize important information.	I can use self-questioning.	I can be ready to solve problems.
I can keep track of my understanding.	I can review vocabulary words to make sure I know what they mean.	I can use my comprehension strategies when I am not sure that I understood what I read.

Access resources, tools, and guides
for this module at the companion website:
resources.corwin.com/howscaffoldingworks

10

PEER SCAFFOLDING

LEARNING INTENTION

We are learning about the ways in which peers can provide scaffolding for one another.

SUCCESS CRITERIA

We will know we are successful when

- We can identify six features of effective scaffolding and how they can be used to provide peer support.
- We can define *emotional scaffolding* and integrate this type of support into peer interactions.
- We can define the helping curriculum and identify moves that create a supportive climate in the classroom.
- We can analyze the different peer tutoring models and identify models that we can implement.

How do you describe peer scaffolds? Use the following questions to jump-start your thinking.

- What training and support might students need to scaffold for one another?

- What type of classroom culture facilitates peer scaffolding?

- How do teachers effectively release responsibility so that peer scaffolding can occur?

We have used the construction metaphor extensively in this book about scaffolding. This is due, in large part, to the choice of the term back in the 1970s when Wood, Bruner, and Ross applied this thinking to education. We have noted the use of external scaffolds applied to buildings and movable scaffolds such as stairs. But there is another type of scaffold: peer support.

Picture the construction scene. We're hanging drywall and using stilts to reach higher places and the ceiling. That's one scaffold, right? We're also using a panel lift to hoist the drywall. Another scaffold. There are probably benches and other supports for the tools and equipment. But it's not really a one-person job. Typically, there are a few people working together, supporting one another as the work gets finished. Thus, the final type of scaffold we'll discuss when it comes to the tasks teachers ask students to complete is **peer scaffolding**. Of course, these tasks need to line up with the expected learning goals, as we noted in an earlier module. But most learning environments have more learners than formal teachers. A typical classroom of 30 to 35 students may have one teacher, and perhaps a co-teacher or assistant. When peers learn to support the learning of others, the number of individuals who can scaffold increases significantly. As Devos (2015) noted, peer scaffolding refers to the "collaborative moves peers make to aid novice others in accomplishing content or linguistic tasks they would otherwise be unable to achieve individually" (p. 147).

There are, of course, formal structures for enacting peer scaffolding. But there are informal processes that naturally occur in classrooms where the climate is focused on learning with widespread recognition that errors are opportunities to learn, rather than a source of shame, humiliation, and embarrassment. In fact, Van Lier (2004) noted six features of effective scaffolding, including

1. **Continuity:** Repeated occurrences over time, with variations connected to one another

2. **Contextual support:** A safe but challenging environment; errors are expected and accepted as part of the learning process

3. **Intersubjectivity:** Mutual engagement and support, two minds thinking as one

4. **Contingency:** The scaffolding support depends on learners' reactions; elements can be added, changed, deleted, repeated, etc.

5. **Handover/takeover:** There is an increasing role for the learner when skills and confidence increase

6. **Flow:** Communication between participants is not forced but flows in a natural way (cited in Khaliliaqdam, 2014, p. 183)

Note that several of these can be effectively delivered by peers. For example, it may be easier for peers to achieve *intersubjectivity*, when two minds are thinking as one, because the student offering scaffolds, having just learned something, is likely to explain it in ways that adults who are more distant from the learning process cannot. Flow might also be easier to achieve when peers are engaged in meaningful conversations with one another.

✳ Use What You Know

Consider the features identified by Van Lier (2004). What are your initial ideas for developing peer supports that rely on each of these? We provided some ideas in the section above, but what ideas do you have?

Scaffolding Feature	Ideas for Mobilizing Peers
Continuity	
Contextual support	
Intersubjectivity	
Contingency	
Handover or takeover	
Flow	

PEER-TO-PEER EMOTIONAL SCAFFOLDING

We introduced emotional scaffolding in Module 2 and noted the ways in which teachers can extend beyond cognitive and metacognitive scaffolds to support students' learning (Nardacchione & Peconio, 2022). Teachers can use "analogies, metaphors, and narratives to influence students' emotional response to specific aspects of the subject matter in a way that promotes student learning" (Rosiek, 2003, p. 402). Meyer and Turner (2007) state that emotional scaffolding includes "temporary but reliable teacher-initiated interactions that support students' positive emotional experiences to achieve a variety of classroom goals" (p. 243).

Teachers, and their actions and behaviors, are an important part of emotional scaffolding. But peers have a profound role to play in the support they can provide to one another. In other words, the teacher can only go so far. There are hundreds, if not thousands, of peer interactions each day that have the potential for good or for harm. As Acar et al. (2017) noted, teacher scaffolding is positively associated with positive peer interactions. If we want to create positive learning environments, we need to enlist peers in supporting one another, and this includes the emotional support necessary to learn.

One example of peer emotional scaffolding involves a schoolwide focus on RULER, developed at the Yale Center for Emotional Intelligence (Yale University, 2022; www.rulerapproach.org). RULER includes five areas: Recognizing, Understanding, Labeling, Expressing, and Regulating emotions. Once each of these has been taught, and students have been given permission to use the tools that have been taught, they can provide emotional scaffolding for one another.

In a middle school class, a group of students were reading *Amal Unbound* (Saeed, 2018). They had been taught several regulation strategies that were used across the school (see Figure 10.1). The book focuses on the life of a girl in rural Pakistan whose mother becomes depressed because she had a girl rather than a boy. The family is in debt and Amal is sent to be a servant until her family can raise enough money. In other words, there are a lot of sensitive and difficult issues to discuss in this book. Unfortunately, during one of their book club sessions, a student said, "Whose mom didn't want you? Mine didn't want me."

Another member of the group started crying, and the students learned that there was a recent death in the family—their peer's mom. This could have turned into an insensitive or awkward situation, but the first student said, "Hey, I'm sorry. This was getting to me, like because my mom left, and my sibs talk about her not wanting us. It's like, how we deal. Do you want to take a break, or should we breathe together and then return? Or maybe we can talk and clarify. I'm open. And I'm really sorry."

A third student added, "I know this sounds kinda weird, but when I get emotional, I want to have a little fun. Like we could play 'Would You Rather?' or something. Or we could talk about our best selves because we all have good things to remember?"

The student whose mom died responded, "I think I need a break. But I do wanna talk about it. I have some connections to this story and now I think I can say them. I didn't want to talk before, but I think I can now."

Of course, this could have gone in a completely different way. But the students in this school had been taught emotional scaffolding, and when push came to shove, they used the skills they had been taught, supporting their peer during a difficult time—and, by the way, maintained their focus on learning (see Figure 10.1).

10.1 REGULATION STRATEGIES

Source: Teacher in Exile (n.d.), https://teacherinexile.com/8-activities-to-scaffold-emotional-regulation-in-the-classroom

COACH A PEER

Park et al. (2020) identified three aspects of emotional scaffolding. For each of these, teachers will need to take action and then support students to scaffold for their peers. We've started a list for you, but your job is to work collaboratively with a peer and add context and actions that will work in your grade level and content area.

ASPECT	EXPLANATION	TEACHER ACTIONS	STUDENT ACTIONS
Create an emotional climate in your classrooms	The climate is how a classroom feels. The classroom must be a safe place to make mistakes and learn. Is this a place where we are all responsible for supporting our own learning and the learning of others?		
Manage students' excitement levels	Teachers need to bring passion to the learning environment and help students develop an intrinsic motivation to learn. Is this a place where learning is exciting and rewarding?		
Maintain students' interest in classroom learning	Students need to see learning and peer interaction and support as relevant. Connections should be made to students' interests and how they learn. Is this a place where I get to learn about myself and things that are valuable?		

PEER SCAFFOLDING THROUGH HELPING

Students can provide the emotional scaffolding that moves learning forward, but it requires a climate that cultivates peer supports. A learning climate that hums with relational trust is one that is more likely to excel. However, students must also be taught how to do so.

Help-seeking is a crucial skill in learning and has an effect size of 0.72, above average in its potential to impact learning (www.visiblelearningmetax.com). The ability to seek help first requires that the student recognize that they have reached an impasse. For instance, a student who has been working on a complex math problem realizes that they have tried everything that they can think of but are now stuck. Another dimension of help-seeking is the social environment. Noticing that one needs help is an indicator of their own self-monitoring.

That same student also considers the social context and decides whether it is psychologically safe to do so. If the student thinks that asking for help will threaten either their social standing (e.g., "My classmates will think I'm dumb") or their reputation with the adult (e.g., "My teacher will think I'm dumb") then they might choose to go it alone or give up. Their goals may also factor into whether they seek help or not. Chou and Chang (2021) write that some students are strategic help-seekers, while others are avoidant:

➤ Strategic help-seekers seek help for learning, as their goals are primarily mastery-driven. ("I need help and I want to learn this.")

➤ Avoidant help-seekers perceive that asking for help is a threat and a sign of failure. ("I don't want anyone to think I can't do this.")

There's much discussion among educators and employers about the "soft skills" needed for learning, employment, and life. Sapon-Shevin (1998) calls it the helping curriculum. She maintains that all people, regardless of age or ability, need to know how to ask for help, offer help, accept help, and politely decline help. Teachers can introduce these principles to students and provide examples and non-examples of each. Students enjoy offering their own stories of each and find it to be a good way to learn more about one another. Figure 10.2 can be used as a reminder of what is required whenever we work with others. Having said that, we recognize that there is a temptation to tell other people the answer. It's quicker for sure. But it does not help. Telling someone "The answer's 24" does not help, but saying "The answer is 24 because . . ." and then engaging in a conversation, such as following up with "How did you figure that out?" is helpful. A classroom climate that promotes help among peers makes it possible to leverage the power of peer scaffolds countless times each day.

10.2   HAVE YOU HELPED TODAY?

Did you offer help?

Did you ask for help?

Did you accept help?

Did you politely decline help so you can try it yourself?

Source: Graphics courtesy of iStock.com/fonikum.

In classrooms where teachers regularly use prompts and cues, as described in Module 8, students begin to use them to help their peers. Interestingly, they don't seem to need to be formally taught to scaffold in this way. It becomes the way that help is provided. It seems that students naturally support the learning of others as they are supported. If the teacher regularly removes the struggle and tells students what they are missing, students begin to do this with their peers. But when teachers prompt and cue, scaffolding the thinking of their students, the students pick this up and begin to do so with their peers.

As an example, a student was having a hard time figuring out which shape was represented by a riddle. Part of the riddle said that the shape had two sides. The unsure student was looking at several shapes, and a peer pointed to the two sides of a cylinder. This gestural cue focused the attention on the student who was not sure and helped the learner process the information. In classrooms where help is not part of the curriculum or where teachers often tell students answers (overhelping), the peer would have probably just told the peer that the answer was a cylinder.

✳ Use What You Know

How can you promote an ethic of helping in your classroom that promotes peer scaffolding? Consider ways that you can create a helping culture in your classroom. Use the chart below to identify ways you are currently promoting a helping culture and places where you'd like to improve.

Promote help-seeking among peers: What techniques do you use? What do you want to cultivate?	
Model how you seek, offer, accept, and politely decline help with students.	
Pause frequently throughout lessons to invite questions.	
Provide times for students to check in with one another about a skill or concept.	
Create student study groups and "study buddies."	

PEER TUTORING

In addition to the emotional support that peers can learn to provide, a more formal model of scaffolding is peer tutoring, which has an effect size of 0.54 on the one receiving the tutoring and an effect size of 0.48 on the one doing the tutoring (visiblelearningmetax.com). Both of these are above-average influences with the potential to accelerate learning. And they are free! Importantly, it's not just the students who receive tutoring who benefit. Part of the value of peer tutoring is impacting the learning of the students who do the tutoring. It's logical to think that tutoring, from teachers, paraprofessionals, or peers, will help others learn. *But* students actually learn more when they have the opportunity to tutor their peers.

There are several different models of peer tutoring, including

Students actually learn more when they have the opportunity to tutor their peers.

➡ *Classwide peer tutoring (CWPT)*. At specific times each week, the class is divided into groups of two to five students. The goal is to practice or review skills and content rather than to introduce new learning. Each student in the group has an opportunity to be both the tutee and the tutor. The teacher typically assigns the content to be covered during these sessions, which includes a peer explaining the work, asking questions of the group, and providing feedback to the peer(s). CWPT involves structured procedures and direct rehearsal and may include competitive teams with the scores posted (Maheady et al., 2001).

➡ *Cross-age peer tutoring*. Older students are paired with younger students and the older students have the responsibility to serve as the tutor. The roles do not change, but the current performance levels of the tutor and tutee may be similar. The tutors explain concepts, model appropriate behavior, ask questions, and encourage better study habits. Tutors may even be taught to design lessons for their younger students (e.g., Jacobson et al., 2001).

➡ *Peer-assisted learning strategies (PALS)*. Pairs of students work together, taking turns tutoring and being tutored. Teachers train students to use the following learning strategies for reading: passage reading with partners, paragraph "shrinking" (or describing the main idea), and prediction relay (predicting what is likely to happen next in the passage) (L. S. Fuchs et al., 1999; D. Fuchs et al., 2000). There are similar procedures for other content areas as well as formal training materials (kc.vanderbilt.edu/pals).

➡ *Same-age peer tutoring*. Like classwide peer tutoring, there are opportunities to create tutoring structures across a grade level or content area (Moliner & Alegre, 2020). In some cases, the same-age peers are within the same classroom, and at other times, they collaborate across classrooms. In same-age tutoring, not all the students are engaged in tutoring at the same time, as would be the case for CWPT. Again, the teacher trains the tutors on their roles and establishes routines for same-age tutoring.

➡ *Reciprocal peer tutoring (RPT)*. In this format of peer tutoring, students are paired at random to support the learning of their peers. It's essentially a collaborative learning task that involves students with similar academic backgrounds working together. Each partnership is responsible for synthesizing content, preparing tasks, and asking questions, complete with answers and explanations. Often students develop practice tests during RPT and then identify areas of additional learning needed (e.g., Alegre-Ansuategui et al., 2017).

➡ *Teach-back*. First discussed as an approach to increase patients' adherence to medical advice (e.g., Ha Dinh et al., 2016), teach-back has been used to solidify PK–12 students' learning as they reframe their learning and teach others (Fisher et al., 2021). Providing students opportunities to teach back what they have learned is good for their learning and it's a great opportunity for determining what has stuck and if there are any misconceptions. And this is not limited to in-class interactions. Students can teach their siblings, parents, or extended family members. They can teach back to the class or directly to the teacher. Notice that teach-back does not require instructional time as it can be conducted outside of class time. Of course, teachers can also arrange time during class for students to teach each other. The key is to ensure that the same students are not always doing the teach-back. Everyone needs an opportunity as it is good for learning and for assessment. Some examples of teach-back follow:

- A student in world history presented on the major events of the labor movement and included quiz questions on a game-based platform throughout the presentation.

- Students in high school geometry taught a lesson to kindergartners about shapes.

- Middle school students took a practice exam in science. Those who scored 70 or below were matched with those who had a passing score for a review of specific items.

- Second graders paired for repeated reading. While the more advanced student read aloud, the other followed with the same text. During the second reading, they engaged in choral reading. During the third reading, the striving student read aloud.

✳ Use What You Know

The following points are useful as you plan and implement a peer tutoring program.

➡ Clarify the specific objectives of the tutoring program, including both academic and social objectives when appropriate.

➡ List objectives in a form that can be easily measured. For example:

- "Students serving as tutees will improve reading fluency by 30% on classroom reading materials in the next 12 weeks."

- "Performance of all students on weekly spelling tests will improve to an average of 85%; no student will score lower than 60%."

➡ Choose tutoring partners carefully. No firm conclusions can be drawn to direct tutoring choices. Some teachers have recommended choosing students as tutors who are conscientious in class, and who generally have to work for their grades. Other considerations include the compatibility of the tutoring pair. Teachers should find pairs who will work together well; however, they should also encourage pairing students who are different in gender, race, or socioeconomic status whenever possible, and not exclusively support established groupings.

➡ Establish rules and procedures for the tutoring program. These rules should cover how students are to interact with each other and specify the type of interactions that are not acceptable. Procedures should specify the times and dates of tutoring, the materials to be used, and the specific activities to be undertaken.

→ Implement the tutoring program, monitor it carefully, and be consistent in enforcing the rules and procedures. Modify rules and procedures as necessary.

→ Evaluate the program frequently, and do not wait until the end of the program to determine whether it was effective. Collect information throughout the program and predict whether it will be successful. If progress is not being made, modify the program.

Source: Mastropieri and Scruggs (2007, p. 183).

Using these points, consider the following questions as you plan peer tutoring as a format of peer scaffolding.

Questions to Consider	My Thinking
1. What are the goals of my peer tutoring program?	
2. Which peer tutoring model(s) will serve me well?	
3. How will I train and support the tutors?	
4. When will tutors do their work? What is the schedule and frequency?	
5. What materials will tutors use?	
6. How will progress and impact be monitored?	

CONCLUSION

In this module, we focused on peer scaffolding. One way that peers can support each other is through emotional scaffolds. In this way, they keep focused on learning as they manage the various emotions that occur throughout the day. In addition, through a helping curriculum and productive classroom climate, peers can use prompts and cues that their teachers model to support the learning of others. And finally, we can formalize peer scaffolding through various models of peer tutoring. In doing so, we can mobilize students to support the learning of others. And, when they do, they learn more. As the French essayist purportedly said, *"To teach is to learn twice."*

SELF-ASSESSMENT

Before moving forward, consider the success criteria for this module. You will notice these statements have been revised from "We can" statements to "Can I?" questions. Using the traffic light scale, with red being not confident, yellow being somewhat confident, and green indicating very confident, how confident are you in your ability to utilize knowledge of peer scaffolds? You'll also want to take note of evidence you have for your self-assessment.

SUCCESS CRITERIA	SELF-ASSESSMENT	EVIDENCE
Can I identify six features of effective scaffolding and how they can be used to provide peer support?		
Can I define *emotional scaffolding* and integrate this type of support into peer interactions?		
Can I define the helping curriculum and identify moves that create a supportive climate in the classroom?		
Can I analyze the different peer tutoring models and identify models that I can implement?		

Access resources, tools, and guides for this module at the companion website: **resources.corwin.com/howscaffoldingworks**

11
FADING SCAFFOLDS

LEARNING INTENTION

We are learning how to fade scaffolds and increase student responsibility and ownership.

SUCCESS CRITERIA

We will know we are successful when

- We can describe automaticity and learned helplessness.
- We can implement wait time strategies to fade scaffolds.
- We can compare and contrast the different types of practice.
- We can decide between least-to-most and most-to-least approaches to scaffolding and fading.

How do you describe fading of the scaffolds that are used to support students? Use the following question stems to jump-start your thinking.

- What is meant by fading?

- What plans might need to be in place to fade scaffolds?

- How might you know if you have faded too quickly?

As we have noted since the beginning of this book, scaffolds are temporary. They are intended to be taken down when the structure underneath is ready. In education, the taking down process is called *fading*, which can occur within a conversation, an activity, a unit, or across the year or course (Martin et al., 2019). Fading involves decreasing the amount or type of scaffolding needed to complete a task or activity. Of course, the goal is for the student to use the skill or concept in a variety of situations, which is known as generalization or transfer.

In fact, we are always in the process of fading scaffolds. This directly relates to practice that we have also discussed over the course of this book.

> Take a moment and list the types of practice we discuss in this playbook.
>
>
>
>
>
> Before moving forward, circle the one that has the greatest potential to move learning forward.

Scaffolds should not be faded before students have acquired the necessary problem-solving processes.

As students engage in deliberate practice, using scaffolds and feedback, they develop habits that endure across time. This is also known as automaticity, or the ability to do things without consciously thinking about them. As LaBerge and Samuels (1974) noted, with practice certain cognitive behaviors could become automatic and thus scaffolding and support for that action would no longer be needed. As Tawfik et al. (2018) stated, "Scaffolds should not be faded before students have acquired the necessary problem-solving processes" (p. 426).

However, if scaffolds are not eventually faded, we run the risk of creating learned helplessness or adult dependency. Students are not born with learned helplessness. Learned helplessness comes from well-meaning adults who provide students with answers rather than having them process the information with scaffolds. Learned helplessness or adult dependency can also happen when we fail to fade the scaffolds. In these cases, students develop a belief that their actions and behaviors do not influence what happens next. In learning, some students believe that they need the support of the teacher to accomplish the tasks and fail to exert sufficient effort to learn. The concept originated with Seligman (1972), who developed the theory to explain a subject's acceptance of their powerlessness, at first by studying how dogs worked in pairs. Our point here is to note that without sufficient fading of scaffolds, students will develop a dependency on the supports provided and fail to reach independence in their learning.

✳ Use What You Know

Revisit the figure that we shared in Module 1. Now that you have explored the various ways that scaffolds and practice can be provided, identify the various contingencies that are required for this model to work.

_____

_____

_____

In addition, note the blue line in Malik's model that identifies the importance of fading. What are your thoughts about the ways in which scaffolds can be faded? Be specific and draw from the context of your own school or classroom.

_____

_____

_____

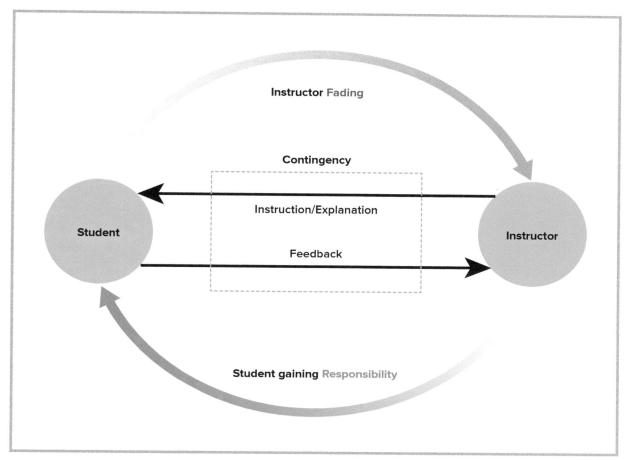

Source: Malik (2017).

There are several different ways to approach fading in our schools and classrooms. We will first look at the role of wait time in fading scaffolds. Then, we will explore least-to-most and most-to-least.

USING WAIT TIME TO FADE SCAFFOLDS

Wait time is the pause you provide a student after you ask an open-ended question, and again after they answer. The pauses allow students some thinking time to contemplate and/or extend the answer. Wait time is a basic principle of teaching, but it's also an important way that we can fade scaffolds. These time delays include a specific amount of time between the instruction and any scaffolds. Typically, we start with no time delay and gradually increase the amount of time between the task and any scaffolding that is provided.

Consider how valuable it is when someone asks you a question that requires some thinking before you respond, and then actually gives you that time. That's wait time. Typically, a wait time of three to eight seconds in length is useful for students to gather their thoughts. In classrooms where the teacher is intentional about wait time, there are a lot fewer "I don't know" replies.

When we are talking, we are filling up students' brain bandwidth (i.e., cognitive load) as they listen and try to understand what is being said. It's only after we stop talking that their thinking can begin. Providing a pause after asking an open-ended question gives students time to think. Pausing after asking an open-ended question is called *Wait Time 1*. But there's also *Wait Time 2*, which is another pause *after* the reply. Students who have provided an answer and then enjoy a few more seconds of quiet will often add to their answer. They use more words, form longer sentences, and give additional ideas. It's great for language development, but also for generating ideas and explanations.

In the space provided, summarize how Wait Time 1 and Wait Time 2 support the fading of scaffolds.

To implement wait time in your own classroom will require deliberate practice. Well, to be honest, you may have to scaffold your own implementation of wait time. That's right! Providing the appropriate wait time is easier said than done. As you think through this way of fading instructional scaffolds, you will likely need to see this done well (mental model), set a goal for yourself (goal setting), and deliberately practice the following techniques. Consider using these techniques when wait time is of value, adapted from advice by educators Wasik and Hindman (2018):

→ *Model waiting and thinking.* When a student asks you a question that requires some thinking on your part, make mention of the fact that you are thinking. "I'm thinking about what you just asked me. I have better answers when I take a few seconds to think."

→ *Teach active listening.* Active listeners focus their attention on the speaker, look at them, and listen quietly for the person to finish. Show students the value of this in your conversations and encourage them when they do so.

→ *Do some silent counting.* Notice the natural pauses you take in discussions with students. You may be surprised to notice that it is as short as one second. Count silently to three or four to help you remember to pause when you're asking an important question or listening to a student respond.

→ *Encourage students to add words and ideas.* Sometimes young people will answer in one word when you were really hoping for more. Asking them to "say more about your idea" can encourage a bit more thinking.

> Make a plan. What is your plan for using wait time in your classroom?

Thus far, we have focused on wait time as an instructional tool that can serve as a scaffold. But wait time can be used to reduce the number of prompts and cues that are provided for students. When we wait, and the climate of the school is supportive of making mistakes and sharing tentative answers, students may engage in more internal processing and share their thinking.

Students in Isabella Ybarra's class were writing descriptive paragraphs. They had success criteria that included having a topic sentence, supporting details, complete sentences, powerful verbs, and a concluding sentence. Ms. Ybarra provided students with a sample paper as a mentor text. She asked her students to identify their topic sentence by highlighting it. Most students did so, and she prompted the four students who did not to find it, which they then did successfully. They then focused on supporting details, asking students to write numbers next to each supporting detail sentence. The four students who had difficulty identifying the topic sentence only numbered one detail sentence.

Ms. Ybarra asked, "Are there more detail sentences?" Ms. Ybarra pointed to a second detail sentence on the copy projected on the wall.

The students all checked their work. She pointed to another detail sentence in the model and the students checked their work.

She then said, "I think we have found three. But maybe there are more. Let's read it again and see if there are any detail sentences." The students did so and some of them identified a fourth detail sentence.

Daniel said to his peers at the table, "I thought we were only supposed to have three." Eliza responded, "Me too. But this one has four and I think it's a good paragraph so maybe we can have more."

"Yeah," Amal added, "I think that's probably right. I could do four or maybe five."

In the meantime, Ms. Ybarra visited with the students who had difficulty with the topic sentence and the detail sentences, checking their work and providing prompts and cues. She decided to then use peer scaffolds and asked students to identify the verbs that they thought were powerful. Once they did, she had them share with others at their table and discuss which verbs they thought were powerful and why.

Ms. Ibarra then decided to fade her scaffolds. She asked the class to identify the concluding sentence, saying, "When you have labeled the concluding sentence, please check that all the sentences are complete, starting with capital letters and ending with appropriate punctuation." As students worked, she walked the room, observing. She noted that most students had identified the concluding sentence and were rereading to focus on complete sentences. She stopped at the table where Mia was working and asked, "Did you identify the concluding sentence?" Mia indicated that she had not. Ms. Ibarra looked back at the paper and then at the student, smiling and pausing without saying anything.

Mia said, "I think it is this one," pointing to the second to the last sentence.

Ms. Ibarra smiled. Mia looked at the paper again and said, "Maybe this is a detail sentence because this one"—pointing to the last one—"is like the first sentence and tells us the topic again." Ms. Ibarra smiled, again without responding. Mia looked back at the paper again. "Yeah, I think that this is the concluding sentence. I'm going to label it. Then I can look at the sentences."

Now that you have read the example from Ms. Ybarra's classroom, go back and circle, underline, or highlight where she used wait time *and* where this reduced the number of prompts and cues.

LEAST-TO-MOST VERSUS MOST-TO-LEAST

There are two ways to think about fading scaffolds: least-to-most or most-to-least. The question is, based on what students are learning, should we start off with the least intensive scaffolds and add them as needed? Or should we begin with the most intensive and back off as students demonstrate success? In large part, this depends on the content or skill to be learned as well as the realities of the classroom as students encounter tasks that challenge them. In other words, this decision depends on the mental model and the specific goals for the learners.

We often increase the amount of scaffolding needed for students to successfully complete a task. In other words, we tend to use a least-to-most approach when it comes to scaffolding. In fact, that was the model of questions, prompts, and cues that we presented in Module 8. For example, a student is working on a math problem and is stuck. We tend to start off with some questions to see if those unlock the student's thinking. If they do not work, we use prompts. And then we might move to cues and even direct explanations. This is an example of least-to-most and allows for natural fading. As students begin to demonstrate increased independence, fewer scaffolds will be necessary.

COACH A PEER

Working alongside a peer, take a moment and recall a situation in your own school or classroom where you increased the amount of scaffolding. Describe the scenario. Focus on the specifics of the scaffolds and the reason for those scaffolds. Use the chart below to document your thinking.

WHAT WERE THE SCAFFOLDS?	WHY DID YOU DECIDE TO INCREASE THE SCAFFOLD? WHAT EVIDENCE LED TO THIS DECISION TO GO FROM LEAST TO MOST?

Importantly, when we use least-to-most approaches to scaffolding, we need to be aware of the need to intentionally fade when students demonstrate success. We also need to determine what might reinforce students such that they take on more of the cognitive load. Grades are a fairly poor reinforcer, and we're not talking about bribing students with candy or other treats. Instead, we need to consider the ways in which we can develop intrinsic motivation with students. In large part, this comes from having goals. We have discussed the values of developing a mental model of expertise in Module 4. That helps build intrinsic motivation and can reduce the amount of scaffolding needed. Reeve and Jang (2006) suggest that there are several ways to develop students' autonomous motivation, including:

➡ Listening to students

➡ Making time for students to work independently

➡ Providing students with an opportunity to talk

➡ Acknowledging improvement and mastery

➡ Encouraging students' effort

➡ Offering hints when students are stuck in order to enable progress

➡ Responding to students' comments and questions

➡ Acknowledging the experiences and perspectives of students

✳ Use What You Know

The Intrinsic Motivation Inventory is a tool used to assess the ways in which students experience tasks. Although it is designed for students, we encourage you to consider a task that you have recently completed, complete the inventory, and then score yourself. Getting familiar with the assessment is useful if you want to use this with students.

	1	2	3	4	5	6	7
	Not at all true			Somewhat true			Very true
While I was working on the task, I was thinking about how much I enjoyed it.							
I did not feel at all nervous about doing the task.							
I felt that it was my choice to do the task.							
I think I am pretty good at this task.							

(Continued)

(Continued)

	1	2	3	4	5	6	7
	Not at all true			Somewhat true			Very true
I found the task very interesting.							
I felt tense while doing the task.							
I think I did pretty well at this activity, compared to other students.							
Doing the task was fun.							
I felt relaxed while doing the task.							
I enjoyed doing the task very much.							
I didn't really have a choice about doing the task.							
I am satisfied with my performance at this task.							
I was anxious while doing the task.							
I thought the task was very boring.							
I felt like I was doing what I wanted to do while I was working on the task.							
I felt pretty skilled at this task.							
I thought the task was very interesting.							
I felt pressured while doing the task.							
I felt like I had to do the task.							
I would describe the task as very enjoyable.							
I did the task because I had no choice.							
After working at this task for a while, I felt pretty competent.							

Source: Center for Self-Determination Theory (n.d.); Ryan and Deci (2000).

Scoring information. Begin by reverse scoring items 2, 9, 11, 14, 19, and 21. In other words, subtract the item response from 8, and use the result as the item score for that item. This way, a higher score will indicate more of the concept described in the sub-scale name. Thus, a higher score on pressure/tension means the person felt more pressured and tense; a higher score on perceived competence means the person felt more competent; and so on. Then calculate subscale scores by averaging the item scores for the items on each subscale. They are as follows. The (R) after an item number is just a reminder that the item score is the reverse of the participant's response to that item.

Interest/enjoyment: 1, 5, 8, 10, 14(R), 17, 20

Perceived competence: 4, 7, 12, 16, 22

Perceived choice: 3, 11(R), 15, 19(R), 21(R)

Pressure/tension: 2(R), 6, 9(R), 13, 18

Having completed this assessment yourself, how might you use this with your students as you think about intrinsic motivation and the ways in which you can fade scaffolds?

PLANNED FADING FROM MOST TO LEAST

As we mentioned earlier, there are two ways to think about fading scaffolds: least-to-most and most-to-least. We recognize that it is more common for teachers to respond on the spot by increasing the level of support they provide for students. Having said that, we note that there are ways to plan scaffolds in advance and intentionally fade them. In this case, we start with the most scaffolding and reduce it as students make progress. In other words, we may start with direct explanations and modeling so that students experience immediate success and build intrinsic motivation. Then we start to fade back as students experience success. This requires very intentional planning and noticing. The risk with this approach is that it goes from most to most and scaffolds are never faded. To intentionally fade the scaffolds, you'll need to identify the criteria for changing the scaffold. This could be a number of days of success, the time in which it takes for the student to experience success, or the developing automaticity that you observe.

For example, as the students were learning skip counting, their teacher Tyler Lewis provided them with a pre-printed page that had the numbers 1 to 25 written with the target number that they were to say printed with dotted lines. For example, 2, 4, 6, and so on were dotted on one page. The students easily completed the task and Mr. Lewis went on to the next one: a page with the numbers missing. When they experienced success with that, he had a board with the 100s chart on it and covered specific numbers with sticky notes. Students completed a close activity in which they provided the missing number and partners could check it by lifting up the sticky note. As he continued to fade the scaffolds, Mr. Lewis provided fewer and fewer supports until students could skip count on their own by 2s. He then repeated the process with the number 5 and so on.

COACH A PEER

Working alongside a peer, take a moment and recall a situation in your own school or classroom where you decreased the amount of scaffolding. Describe the scenario. Focus on the specifics of the scaffolds and the reason for those scaffolds. Use the chart below to document your thinking.

WHAT WERE THE SCAFFOLDS?	WHY DID YOU DECIDE TO DECREASE THE SCAFFOLD? WHAT EVIDENCE LED TO THIS DECISION TO GO FROM MOST TO LEAST?

CONCLUSION

Consider the two charts you completed in this module: least-to-most and most-to-least. Looking at your responses to both of these tasks, you likely see connections between the two approaches. Fading instructional scaffolds requires us to pull together all other aspects of our model. The mental model tells us the endpoint for fading. The goal setting helps us clarify whether to move from least to most or most to least. The nature of the task, along with front-end, distributed, back-end, and peer scaffolding, guides us in deciding what, specifically is faded. Feedback informs the timing of that fade.

Fading takes us back to the very start of this playbook. The impressive construction of the RCA building in the 1930s required scaffolds to go from the ground floor all the way up to the sixty-sixth story. This 850-foot-tall building, while not the tallest in Manhattan, New York, is nonetheless an impressive structure when you think about the time period in which it was built and where this building was constructed. Scaffolding made this impressive feat go from a blueprint to a historic building. While we are not constructing skyscrapers in our classrooms, we are writing a narrative essay, analyzing primary and secondary sources, balancing oxidation-reduction reactions, adding two fractions with unlike denominators, blending watercolors, or overhand throwing. These complex tasks require scaffolding.

However, if you see the RCA building today, now called Rockefeller Plaza, there is no longer scaffolding around that building. When the construction was done, the goals met, and the mental model (i.e., blueprint) achieved, the construction workers removed the scaffolding for all to see the finished product. Scaffolds are part of the process, not the product. The same goes for the complex tasks in our classrooms. Scaffolds need to be removed—faded—so that students develop independence. There is limited research on how this happens. In fact, a library search on fading scaffolds results in very few studies. What we do know is that it needs to be done if students are going to be able to transfer their learning beyond the immediate setting in which they are learning. Wait time is one way that we can fade scaffolds. In addition, we can be intentional with our plans to fade based on the approach we have taken, starting with either the most intensive scaffolds or the least intensive. Unlike a building, which we have used metaphorically throughout this book, educational scaffolds are probably much more flexible, coming and going across lessons, units, and weeks as students work on the tasks that they are assigned.

SELF-ASSESSMENT

Before moving forward, consider the success criteria for this module. You will notice these statements have been revised from "We can" statements to "Can I?" questions. Using the traffic light scale, with red being not confident, yellow being somewhat confident, and green indicating very confident, how confident are you in your ability to fade scaffolds? You'll also want to take note of evidence you have for your self-assessment.

SUCCESS CRITERIA	SELF-ASSESSMENT	EVIDENCE
Can I describe automaticity and learned helplessness?	●━━━━━━━●	
Can I implement wait time strategies to fade scaffolds?	●━━━━━━━●	
Can I compare and contrast the different types of practice?	●━━━━━━━●	
Can I decide between least-to-most and most-to-least approaches to scaffolding and fading?	●━━━━━━━●	

Access resources, tools, and guides
for this module at the companion website:
resources.corwin.com/howscaffoldingworks

Conclusion

So, How Does Scaffolding Work?

To ensure all learners have equitable access and opportunity to the highest level of learning possible, we must recognize that the learning journey for each student will be different. However, that difference should not, must not, and cannot be in the complexity of thinking, the rigor of the learning experience, or expectations in outcomes. The difference should be, must be, and can be in the instructional scaffolds that provide the necessary support system or structure that provides equitable access and opportunity. Flip back to the very first words in this playbook: we were very clear in the characteristics of instructional scaffolds. This supporting framework is temporary and movable, allowing individuals to move forward in whatever task is at hand. Let's review the three big ideas of instructional scaffolding.

1. Scaffolding is only used when the task at hand is not possible to complete without that support system or structure.

2. Scaffolding is customized (i.e., movable) based on the specific needs of the individuals engaged in the task; there is no one-size-fits-all scaffolding.

3. Scaffolding is used until the support system or structure is no longer needed; scaffolds are temporary and not permanent.

When asked *How does scaffolding work?*, consider that the answer depends on the task, the learners, and how long the learner needs the scaffold for the task. The importance of this relationship cannot be overstated. In fact, let's put this into a mathematical relationship. Take a look at the relationships below and fill in the missing variables. There is a word bank on the next page to scaffold your learning.

If _____ > _____, then the

outcome = _____ and _____.

If _____ < _____, then the

outcome = _____ and _____.

If _____ = _____, then the

outcome = _____ and _____.

Word Bank (words may be used more than once)

Scaffolding

Need

Learned helplessness

Dependency

Frustration

Disengagement

Learning

Engagement

Learned helplessness and dependency come from scaffolds that exceed the needs of the learners. Frustration and disengagement come from too little scaffolding. The right balance leads to learning and engagement.

Visit the Visible Learning Meta^X website (www.visiblelearningmetax.com). Locate the effect size for scaffolding and write it in the space below.

Effect Size for Scaffolding: _____

Then locate the effect size for student-teacher dependency, learned helplessness, and frustration. Write those effect sizes in the spaces below.

Effect Size for Teacher-Student Dependency: _____

Effect Size for Learned Helplessness: _____

Effect Size for Frustration: _____

Finally, locate the effect size for "the right level of challenge." Write that in the space below.

Effect Size for Right Level of Challenge: _____

The story is in the data. Instructional scaffolds help us to design and implement learning experiences that are the right level of challenge for our learners.

Over the past 11 modules, we have tried to unpack what this looks like in practice. Whether you are teaching kindergarten or chemistry, physical education or physics, second graders or seniors in high school, moving scaffolding from an effect size to an effective way to support learners is absolutely necessary if we are going to move from research to reality. The model for *how scaffolding words* allows us to make that move. As our final task, fill in the model below with the contingencies for instructional scaffolding.

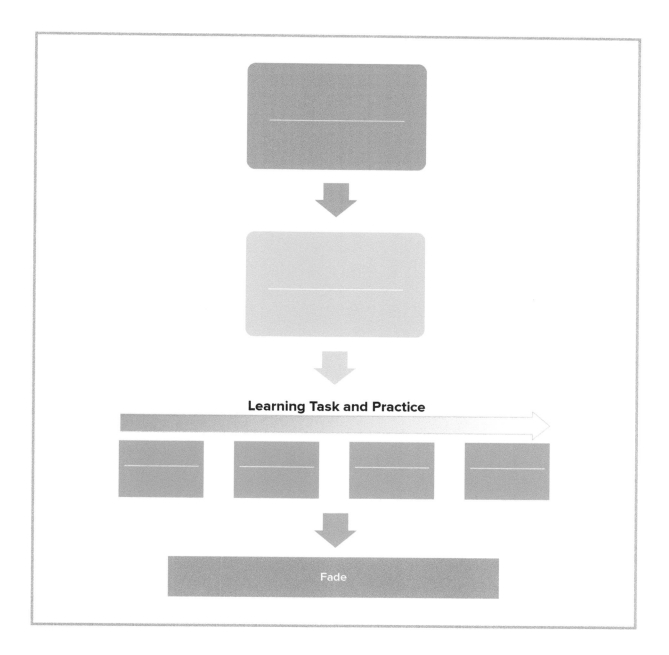

Even if you had to flip back through the playbook to find the concepts that go into this model, that is a good start. To support your scaffolding journey, we have provided a template to help guide the discussion you have with your PLC+ team, content area team, grade-level planning team, or instructional coach. Your accountability partner or team is vital in working through the scaffolding process.

A Plan for Scaffolding

Learning Task: _____

Mental Models

- What are the essential concepts, skills, and understandings needed to demonstrate proficiency or mastery?
- What are the nonessential aspects of this learning task that can be left for the learner to decide?
- How will I communicate the mental model?

Goal Setting

- What evidence do I need to determine where my learners are in their progression toward the mental model?
- How will I set aside time with my learners to set goals and develop a plan?
- How will I monitor or track progress toward the goals?

Learning Task

| What front-end scaffolds are needed to support learners in engaging in the learning task? | What scaffolds will be distributed throughout the learning task? | How can I or would I use peer scaffolding during the learning task? | How will I know what back-end scaffolds are needed to support learners in engaging in the learning task? |

What is my plan for fading the scaffolds?

Scaffolding is a process. Making continuous adjustments along the way ensures we have the right level of challenge that moves learning forward and maximizes active engagement. In addition, scaffolding increases student agency and efficacy. Truly successful scaffolding builds capacity in learners so that they know what to do when they don't know what to do, and we are not their teachers anymore.

As we close out this playbook, we want to solicit some feedback from you. Use the space below to answer the question we have been working on for the last 163 pages: *How does scaffolding work?*

Yes, the answer may need some scaffolds of its own. But making the commitment to scaffold learning for ourselves and in our own schools and classrooms is worth it!

Now, let's get to it!

References

Acar, I. H., Hong, S., & Wu, C. (2017). Examining the role of teacher presence and scaffolding in preschoolers' peer interactions. *European Early Childhood Education Research Journal, 25*(6), 866–884.

Alegre-Ansuategui, F. J., Moliner, L., Lorenzo, G., & Maroto, A. (2017). Peer tutoring and academic achievement in mathematics: A meta-analysis. *Eurasia Journal of Mathematics, Science and Technology Education, 14*, 337–354.

Alfassi, M. (2004). Reading to learn: The effects of combined strategies instruction on high school students. *Journal of Educational Research, 97*(4), 171–184.

Almarode, J., Fisher, D., & Frey, N. (2023). *How feedback works: A playbook*. Corwin.

Almarode, J., Fisher, D., Thunder, K., & Frey, N. (2021). *The success criteria playbook: A hands-on guide to making learning visible*. Corwin.

Anderson, N. J. (2002). *The role of metacognition in second language teaching and learning*. ERIC Clearinghouse on Language and Linguistics. https://www.cal.org/publications/the-role-of-metacognition-in-second-language-teaching-and-learning/

August, D., Branum-Martin, L., Cardenas-Hagan, E., & Francis, D. J. (2009). The impact of an instructional intervention on the science and language learning of middle grade English language learners. *Journal of Research on Educational Effectiveness, 2*, 345–376.

Ausubel, D. P. (1968). *Educational psychology: A cognitive view*. Holt, Rinehart, & Winston.

Block, M. E. (1995). Use peer tutors and task sheets. *Strategies, 9*(4), 9–12.

Browne, A. (2001). *Voices in the park*. DK Publishing.

Buehl, D. (2017). Text prep. *Educational Leadership, 74*(5), 60–65.

CAST. (2018). *Universal design for learning guidelines version 2.2*. http://udlguidelines.cast.org

Cazden, C. B. (2001). *Classroom discourse: The language of teaching and learning* (2nd ed.). Heinemann.

Center for Self-Determination Theory. (n.d.). *Intrinsic motivation inventory (IMI)*. https://selfdeterminationtheory.org/intrinsic-motivation-inventory/

Chou, C. Y., & Chang, C. H. (2021). Developing adaptive help-seeking regulation mechanisms for different help-seeking tendencies. *Educational Technology & Society, 24*(4), 54–66.

Contrera, J. (2019). One of the most iconic photos of American workers is not what it seems. *The Washington Post*. https://www.washingtonpost.com/history/2019/09/01/one-most-iconic-photos-american-workers-is-not-what-it-seems

Covey, S. (1995). *First things first*. Simon and Schuster.

Cuba, M. J. (2020). Frontloading academic vocabulary for English learners with disabilities in an integrated classroom setting. *Intervention in School & Clinic, 55*(4), 230–237.

Devos, N. J. (2015). *Peer interactions in new content and language-integrated settings*. Springer International Publishing.

Dixon, J. (2018). *Providing scaffolding just in case*. http://www.dnamath.com/blog-post/five-ways-we-undermine-efforts-to-increase-student-achievement-and-what-to-do-about-it-part-3-of-5/

Dutro, S., & Moran, C. (2003). Rethinking English language instruction: An architectural approach. In G. Garcia (Ed.), *English learners: Reaching the highest level of English literacy* (pp. 227–258). International Reading Association.

EL Education. (n.d.). *Helping all learners: Scaffolding*. https://eleducation.org/resources/helping-all-learners-scaffolding

Englert, C. S., & Mariage, T. V. (1991). Making students partners in the comprehension process: Organizing the reading POSSE. *Learning Disability Quarterly, 14*, 123–138.

Ericsson, A., & Pool, R. (2016). *Peak: Secrets from the new science of expertise*. Houghton Mifflin Harcourt.

Expeditionary Learning. (2013). *Meeting students' needs through scaffolding*. Author.

Fisher, D., & Frey, N. (2013). *Better learning through structured teaching: A framework for the gradual release of responsibility* (2nd ed.). ASCD.

Fisher, D., & Frey, N. (2017). Teaching study skills. *The Reading Teacher, 71*, 373–378.

Fisher, D., & Frey, N. (2018). The uses and misuses of graphic organizers in content area learning. *The Reading Teacher, 71*(6), 763–766.

Fisher, D., Frey, N., Almarode, J., Flories, K., & Nagel, D. (2020). *PLC+: Better decisions and greater impact by design.* Corwin.

Fisher, D., Frey, N., Smith, D., & Hattie, J. (2021). *Rebound: A playbook for rebuilding agency, accelerating learning recovery, and rethinking schools.* Corwin.

Frey, N., & Fisher, D. (2010). Identifying instructional moves during guided learning. *The Reading Teacher, 64*, 84–95.

Frey, N., Hattie, J., & Fisher, D. (2018). *Developing assessment-capable visible learners, grades K–12: Maximizing skill, will, and thrill.* Corwin.

Fuchs, D., Fuchs, L., & Burish, P. (2000). Peer-assisted learning strategies: An evidence-based practice to promote reading achievement. *Learning Disabilities Research and Practice, 15*(2), 85–91.

Fuchs, L. S., Fuchs, D., & Kazdan, S. (1999). Effects of peer-assisted learning strategies on high school students with serious reading problems. *Remedial and Special Education, 20*(5), 309–318.

Ha Dinh, T. T., Bonner, A., Clark, R., Ramsbotham, J., & Hines, S. (2016). The effectiveness of the teach-back method on adherence and self-management in health education for people with chronic disease: A systematic review. *JBI Database of Systematic Reviews and Implementation, 14*(1), 210–247.

Hastie, P. A., Rudisill, M. E., & Wadsworth, D. D. (2013). Providing students with voice and choice: Lessons from intervention research on autonomy-supportive climates in physical education. *Sport, Education & Society, 18*(1), 38–56.

Hattie, J. (2009). *Visible learning: A synthesis of over 800 meta-analyses relating to achievement.* Routledge.

Hattie, J., & Clark, S. (2019). *Visible learning feedback.* Routledge.

Hoover, J. J., & Patton, P. R. (1995). *Teaching students with learning problems to use study skills: A teacher's guide.* Pro-Ed.

Iris Center. (n.d.). *What is instructional scaffolding?* https://iris.peabody.vanderbilt.edu/module/sca/cresource/q1/p01/

Jacobson, J., Thrope, L., Fisher, D., Lapp, D., Frey, N., & Flood, J. (2001). Cross-age tutoring: A literacy improvement approach for struggling adolescent readers. *Journal of Adolescent and Adult Literacy, 44*, 528–536.

Kapur, M. (2016). Examining productive failure, productive success, unproductive failure, and unproductive success in learning. *Educational Psychologist, 51*(2), 289–299.

Kapur, M. (2019, September 28). *Productive failure. TEDx Lugano.* https://www.manukapur.com/prof-manu-kapur-at-tedx-lugano-sep-28-2019/

Khaliliaqdam, S. (2014). ZPD, scaffolding, and basic speech development in EFL context. *Procedia: Social and Behavioral Sciences, 98*, 891–897.

LaBerge, D., & Samuels, S. J. (1974). Toward a theory of automatic information processing in reading. *Cognitive Psychology, 6*(2), 293–323.

Lesaux, N. K., Kieffer, M. J., Kelley, J. G., & Harris, J. R. (2014). Effects of academic vocabulary instruction for linguistically diverse adolescents: Evidence from a randomized field trial. *American Educational Research Journal, 51*, 1159–1194.

Lowry, L. (1993). *The giver.* Houghton Mifflin.

Maheady, L., Harper, G. F., & Mallette, B. (2001). Peer-mediated instruction and interventions and students with mild disabilities. *Remedial and Special Education, 22*, 4–15.

Malik, S. A. (2017). Revisiting and re-representing scaffolding: The two-gradient model. *Cogent Education, 4*(1), 1331533. https://doi.org/10.1080/2331186X.2017.1331533

Martin, N. D., Dornfeld Tissenbaum, C., Gnesdilow, D., & Puntambekar, S. (2019). Fading distributed scaffolds: The importance of complementarity between teacher and material scaffolds. *Instructional Science, 47*, 69–98.

Mastropieri, M. A., & Scruggs, T. E. (2007). *The inclusive classroom: Strategies for effective instruction* (3rd ed.). Merrill/Prentice Hall.

Menninga, A., van Geert, P., van Vondel, S., Steenbeek, H., & van Dijk, M. (2022). Teacher-student interaction patterns change during an early science teaching intervention. *Research in Science Education, 52*, 1497–1523.

Meyer, D. K., & Turner, J. C. (2007). Scaffolding emotions in classrooms. In P. A. Schutz & R. Pekrun (Eds.), *Emotion in education* (pp. 243–258). Elsevier Academic Press.

Miner, H. (1956). Body ritual among the Nacirema. *American Anthropologist, 58*(3), 503–507.

Moll, L. (1990). Introduction. In L. C. Moll (Ed.), *Vygotsky and education: Instructional implications and applications of sociohistorical psychology* (pp. 1–27). Cambridge University Press.

Moliner, L., & Alegre, F. (2020). Effects of peer tutoring on middle school students' mathematics self-concepts. *PLoS One, 15*(4), e0231410. https://doi.org/10.1371/journal.pone.0231410

Nardacchione, G., & Peconio, G. (2022). Peer tutoring and scaffolding principle for inclusive teaching. *Elementa, 1*(1–2), 181–200.

Nottingham, J. A. (2017). *The learning challenge: How to guide your students through the learning pit to achieve deeper understanding.* SAGE.

Nuthall, G. (2007). *The hidden lives of learners.* NZCER Press.

Palincsar, A. S., & Brown, A. L. (1986). Interactive teaching to promote independent learning from text. *The Reading Teacher, 39*(8), 771–777.

Park, M., Tiwari, A., & Neumann, J. W. (2020). Emotional scaffolding in early childhood education. *Educational Studies, 46*(5), 570–589.

Puntambekar, S. (2022). Distributed scaffolding: Scaffolding students in classroom environments. *Educational Psychology Review, 34*, 451–472.

Puntambekar, S., & Kolodner, J. L. (2005). Toward implementing distributed scaffolding: Helping students learn science from design. *Journal of Research in Science Teaching, 42*(2), 185–217.

Reeve, J., & Jang, H. (2006). What teachers say and do to support students' autonomy during a learning activity. *Journal of Educational Psychology, 98*(1), 209–218.

Rosiek, J. (2003). Emotional scaffolding: An exploration of the teacher knowledge at the intersection of student emotion and the subject matter. *Journal of Teacher Education, 54*(5), 399–412.

Ryan, P. M. (2002). *Esperanza rising.* Scholastic.

Ryan, R., & Deci, E. (2000). Self-determination theory and the facilitation of intrinsic motivation, social development, and well-being. *American Psychologist, 55*(1), 68–78.

Saeed, A. (2018). *Amal unbound.* Penguin Random House.

Sapon-Shevin, M. (1998). *Because we can change the world: A practical guide to building cooperative, inclusive classroom communities.* Allyn & Bacon.

Searle, D. (1984). Scaffolding: Who's building whose building? *Language Arts, 61*(5), 480–483.

Seligman, M. E. (1972). Learned helplessness. *Annual Review of Medicine, 23*(1), 407–412.

Sweller, J. (1988). Cognitive load during problem solving: Effects on learning. *Cognitive Science, 12*(2), 257–285.

Tajeddin, Z., & Kamali, J. (2020). Typology of scaffolding in teacher discourse: Large data-based evidence from second language classrooms. *International Journal of Applied Linguistics, 30*(2), 329–343.

Tawfik, A., Law, V., Ge, X., Xing, W., & Kim, K. (2018). The effect of sustained vs. faded scaffolding on students' argumentation in ill-structured problem solving. *Computers in Human Behavior, 87*, 436–449.

Teacher in Exile. (n.d.). *RULER: Classroom activities for social-emotional learning.* https://teacherinexile.com/8-activities-to-scaffold-emotional-regulation-in-the-classroom

Thompson, I. (2009). Scaffolding in the writing center: A microanalysis of an experienced tutor's verbal and nonverbal tutoring strategies. *Written Communication, 26*(4), 417–453.

Time, Inc. (2016). *100 photographs: The most influential images of all time.* Time Incorporated Books.

Tjeerdsma, B. L. (1995). How to motivate students . . . without standing on your head! *Journal of Physical Education, Recreation, and Dance, 66*(5), 36–39.

van de Pol, J., Volman, M., & Beishuizen, J. (2010). Scaffolding in teacher-student interaction: A decade of research. *Educational Psychology Review, 22*(3), 271–296.

Van Lier, L. (2004). *The ecology and semiotics of language learning.* Kluwer Academic Press.

Vrabie, D. (2021). *The three forms of feedback: Appreciation, coaching, and evaluation.* CTO Craft. https://ctocraft.com/blog/the-three-forms-of-feedback-appreciation-coaching-and-evaluation/

Wasik, B., & Hindman, A. (2018). Why wait? The importance of wait time in developing young students' language and vocabulary skills. *The Reading Teacher, 72*(3), 369–378.

Wood, D. (1998). How *children think and learn: The social contexts of cognitive development* (2nd ed.). Blackwell.

Wood, D., Bruner, J. S., & Ross, G. (1976). The role of tutoring in problem solving. *Journal of Child Psychology and Psychiatry, 17*(2), 89–100.

Woodson, J. (2016). *Brown girl dreaming.* Puffin Books.

Yale University. (2022). RULER approach. *Yale Center for Emotional Intelligence.* https://www.rulerapproach.org/

Index

> **Every student deserves a great teacher—not by chance, but by design.**

Read more from Fisher & Frey

Learn to create a culture of feedback in your classroom with the latest research on teaching, engagement, and assessment with this concise and interactive playbook.

Rich with resources that support the process of parlaying scientific findings into classroom practice, this playbook offers all the moves teachers need to design learning experiences that work for all students.

This easy-to-use playbook prompts educators to clarify, articulate, and actualize instructional leadership goals with the aim of delivering on the promise of equity and excellence for all.

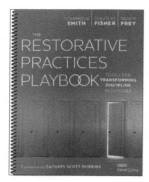

Transform negative behavior into a teachable moment at your school, utilizing restorative practices that are grounded in relationships and a commitment to the well-being of others.

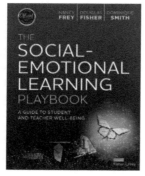

This interactive playbook provides the language, moves, and evidence-based advice you need to nurture social and emotional learning in yourself, your students, and your school.

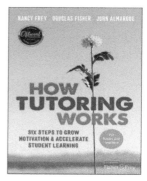

Harnessing decades of Visible Learning® research, this easy-to-read, eye-opening guide details the six essential components of effective tutoring.

To order your copies, visit corwin.com/FisherandFrey

CORWIN
A SAGE Publishing Company

CORWIN HAS ONE MISSION: to enhance education through intentional professional learning.

We build long-term relationships with our authors, educators, clients, and associations who partner with us to develop and continuously improve the best evidence-based practices that establish and support lifelong learning.